MORE GREAT
DOG STORIES

MORE GREAT DOG STORIES

Inspirational Tales About Exceptional Dogs

ROXANNE WILLEMS SNOPEK

VICTORIA · VANCOUVER · CALGARY

Heritage House Publishing Company Ltd.
www.heritagehouse.ca

Library and Archives Canada Cataloguing in Publication
Snopek, Roxanne Willems
    More great dog stories: inspirational tales about exceptional dogs/
Roxanne Willems Snopek.—1st Heritage House ed.

(Amazing stories)
ISBN 978-1-894974-57-8

    1. Working dogs—Anecdotes. I. Title. II. Series.

SF428.2.S56 2008   636.73   C2008-905641-8

Also available in e-pub format, ISBN 978-1-926613-82-6

Edited by Lesley Reynolds.
Proofread by Karla Decker.
Cover design by Chyla Cardinal. Interior design by Frances Hunter.
Cover photo by Leigh Schindler/iStockphoto. Interior photos by Tim Sundstrom, page 29; Doris Seelig, page 51; Anna Lupacchino, pages 69 and 80; Gwen and Carl Dingee, page 107; Darci Kitt, page 121; Stephanie Snopek, page 133.

MIX
Paper from
responsible sources
FSC   FSC® C016245
www.fsc.org

The interior of this book was produced using 100% post-consumer recycled paper, processed chlorine free and printed with vegetable-based inks.

Heritage House acknowledges the financial support for its publishing program from the Government of Canada through the Canada Book Fund (CBF), Canada Council for the Arts and the province of British Columbia through the British Columbia Arts Council and the Book Publishing Tax Credit.

Canada Council   Conseil des Arts
for the Arts   du Canada

BRITISH COLUMBIA
ARTS COUNCIL
Supported by the Province of British Columbia

13 12 11 10   2 3 4 5
Printed in Canada

Contents

Prologue

BESIDE THE ARMCHAIR IN MY *writing room, in the basket beneath the window, lies a black poodle named Myshkin. To the untrained eye, he appears to be asleep. He is not. He is waiting. He knows that eventually I'll close my laptop computer and get up. When I do, he springs to his feet, ears cocked in anticipation, ready to join me in whatever fun I might be having.*

When he arrived three years ago, I could barely get out of bed, let alone house-train a puppy. I'd just had major surgery, and the practical decision would have been to defer getting my puppy until I'd fully recovered. By the time I'd gotten the news that surgery was required, however, I was already getting regular update photos from the breeder. I saw "my" puppy as a newborn. I knew which day his eyes opened, and saw pictures of him and his littermates peering over the edge of the whelping box. It was far too late to change my mind by then.

I didn't know that I was about to enter a dark, fallow period, a shadow-filled valley from which I couldn't seem to escape. Many times when I felt utterly alone, my small, curly-coated companion would push his black nose into my hand, insistently leading me to the one thing that could help.

"Come on," his sparkling eyes urged me. "Let's play!"

1

Jailhouse Dogs

IN 1989, WHEN KATHY GIBSON drove through the gates of the Lakeside Correctional Centre for Women in Burnaby, British Columbia, she had no idea what lay before her. Inside those gates were hard-core women, convicted criminals, some of whom had been locked away time after time, seemingly determined to reject the rules of life outside an institution. Kathy had been asked to help devise a program for these inmates, using dogs. She had no idea how— or even if—a canine program could help these women. A long-time animal behaviourist, Kathy had no shortage of ideas; what she lacked was data on animal-facilitated therapy programs in prison.

"No one had any idea what the program would or could

be," she says. "I was excited, exhilarated to be taking on something no one had done before in Canada."

Kathy had worked with dogs in one way or another most of her life, but it wasn't until 1981, when she met her husband, Gary, that she thought of doing it professionally. "He's more business-minded than I am," she says. "He suggested doing it as a business, full-time." So the two of them did just that. They ran classes for dog owners, taught seminars in special-interest areas, consulted on behaviour problems like aggression and fear-biting, and developed therapy programs. Eventually they helped found a non-profit organization they called the British Columbia Society for Human-Animal Interaction. Its purpose was to establish training standards for volunteers doing pet visitation and in animal-assisted therapy programs. Although the Gibsons are no longer involved in the organization (now called British Columbia Pets and Friends), it was while Kathy was involved in this society that the correctional institution approached her.

Since nothing like this had ever been done in Canada, everyone had a different opinion on how it should be run (or even whether it should be run at all). Not only were there no guidelines, there were also no preconceived notions. But Kathy persevered. She believed this was a chance to use her gut instinct and experience to create something wonderful out of nothing. The model they ended up with was a very loosely structured plan for having inmates socialize unadoptable, last-chance shelter dogs to the point where the animals could be placed in permanent homes.

"That really was the only idea I went into the prison with," Kathy says. "I didn't have any concrete plans." It didn't take long for her ideas to solidify. They called the initiative "Canine Corrections."

A small building on the prison grounds served as her base of operations. It housed a kennel with indoor runs and a fenced yard for exercise and training. Inmates had to apply to participate in the program, and they had to adhere to a strict code of behaviour in order to stay in it. "I had the right to hire and fire inmates for the program, and if they screwed up, they were out," says Kathy. "Our inmates had to be above reproach because, although many were very supportive, some of the administrators and staff members were looking for any reason to shut down the program."

The women who were involved showed up at the kennel each day, just like they would have done for a regular job. The first few weeks were a revelation to Kathy. Problem dogs she understood; she could see the fear in their eyes and recognize the unmet needs beneath the inappropriate behaviour. But she had a lot to learn about women convicts. Then it hit her: these incarcerated women were not so different from many of the so-called "problem" dogs she encountered. "Federal, long-term prisoners are different from the rotating-door prisoners, the drug users who are in and out all the time," she says. "They've had such bad backgrounds, such horrible experiences."

She learned that the vast majority of them had been subjected to some form of physical, emotional, mental and/or sexual abuse. Most of them also had substance-abuse issues. Almost all of them had difficulty forming healthy relationships. How could they live normal lives when they didn't even know what that meant? Understanding and sympathy, however, only go so far. "They are victims," says Kathy, "but you can't treat them like victims. Instead, you have to give them the skills they need to succeed."

At the time, Kathy was frustrated with a great deal of what was happening in the world of dog training. She saw people using excessive force to dominate dogs when dominance was not the issue. She saw punishment and reward being used without results. And she saw a lot of frustrated owners and misunderstood dogs. "I was working in shelters where I was seeing scared, scared, scared dogs that were being treated really negatively," she says. "When you're dealing with behaviour problems, it's *always* about fear and lack of control, all the time." For her, the challenge was to look deeper into the dog's life, find out about the family and the household and figure out *why* the dog was acting inappropriately.

This, she decided, was what she wanted to emphasize to the women in her program. Little by little, the Canine Corrections program began to take shape. Kathy felt it was important for the focus to stay entirely on the dogs, not the women, but the women could earn the right to participate in decisions made about the dogs. And they would be given a measure of control, something they'd lost long ago. "The institution is all hierarchical, top-down, with the inmates at the bottom," says Kathy. But the Canine Corrections program provided inmates a chance to actually be rewarded for putting someone else first. And, in the long run, all the things they had to do to help the dogs—be consistent, show up on time, control their tempers, be good leaders, be kind and so on—were things they needed to learn for their own benefit.

The dogs Canine Corrections brought in were animals the shelters had given up on. Often they were only hours away from being euthanized. "These were dogs with a lot of issues," says Kathy, "and the women identified with them because they'd all been told they were losers, too." Each woman was given the responsibility of building a relationship with the dog; training was less of a priority. "Once I understood what the inmates' concerns were, I looked through a lot of shelters, then picked a 'short list' of dogs I thought might fit well, or whose needs meshed with issues an inmate might have repressed. But I didn't always know which dog would be right for each inmate. Once the dogs were chosen, I just pushed open the door and let the dogs and the women find each other.

"The inmates went through the same stages that the dogs did," says Kathy. "They all started by trying to find out: 'Are you safe? Can I trust you? Will you try to manipulate me?'" Trust, the very foundation of every relationship, was the first hurdle to conquer, for both the women and their dogs. "They learned to look at themselves and their issues by looking at the dogs. When they caught on, they could look at things from a different perspective. The women were just as misunderstood as the dogs."

Kathy insisted on keeping the focus on the dogs. "When the women joined the program, I didn't know what they'd done, and I didn't care," she says. "I told them, 'All I know is how you take care of the dog.'" As part of the program, participants had to create plans for helping their dogs, carry out those plans and write progress reports. If they didn't carry out their responsibilities, or if they broke the kennel rules, they were kicked out. They were always allowed to earn their way back in, if they made proper restitution, but Kathy knew they had to recognize that even though she wasn't part of the institution, they had to do as she said, for the good of the dogs. "The women learned that they were the authors of their own destinies," she says. Instead of rules for the sake of rules, or for the convenience of someone else, or just as a show of power, Kathy's rules were for the sake of the dogs. This was an empowering revelation for these women.

One of the first dogs brought into the Canine Corrections experiment was Gizmo, a pathetic little Lhasa Apso that Kathy's husband Gary had found huddled in the corner of a shelter, terrified, dirty and completely matted. They shaved him down, cleaned him up and brought him into the program. But Gizmo had his own agenda. "Dogs weren't allowed inside Lakeside except during specific pet visitation times, which would have been scheduled, supervised and controlled," explains Kathy. "Gizmo was sneaking in on his own." Small enough to fit through the barred doors, Gizmo quickly learned where the staff members kept their lunches and took every chance he could to slip away from the kennel, run inside the prison and steal a snack. When anyone in a uniform tried to catch him, he bared his tiny fangs. "Gizmo was always breaking into the institution," says Kathy, laughing. "He had a great time. The guards would have to go call an inmate to rescue their lunch!"

As the program progressed, people across the country heard about it. One day a woman named Jane, a long-term prisoner in Kingston Penitentiary, asked to be transferred to Lakeside so she could participate in Canine Corrections. "She was such a hopeless case that the administration figured, 'Why not?' and shipped her out," recalls Kathy.

Kathy didn't even know where to start with Jane. "She was a very slow learner." She was also illiterate and barely spoke." Kathy had a list of 10 rules that she insisted everyone know and understand, so she told Jane that until she could write down the rules, she couldn't be a full participant in the program. She could be with them in the kennel and watch and help the other inmates, but she wouldn't be given a dog of her own to work with until she met this requirement.

Jane was in her late 30s, and during her many years in prison had never been willing to attend literacy classes. Now she had a reason. She began working with a teacher, going through the painful process of learning something most of us take for granted every single day of our lives. Finally she was ready. "I'll never forget the day she went up to the flip chart and wrote down the rules," says Kathy. "She was so proud! It took her an hour, but she got all 10."

She was ready to work with her own dog. Jane was paired with Fluffy, a little white poodle-cross dog that had been rescued from a puppy mill. "He was just a mess," says Kathy. "He was scared and so badly matted we could have made a small sweater out of what we shaved off." They started working together, going through the ordinary motions of feeding, grooming, going for walks in the field and meeting other people. Throughout these seemingly ordinary tasks, the two of them were experiencing a life of consistency and safety.

Jane always showed up on time and did her tasks well. And Fluffy seemed to respond to her. But neither of them looked happy. Jane clumped around the field silently, with no sign of emotion on her face. Fluffy followed her, his tail down, his ears folded back anxiously, as if expecting disaster. One day Kathy told Jane that she needed to help Fluffy become happy. The woman looked at her, stumped. "She said, 'I don't laugh,'" says Kathy. "And I said, 'I know. What are we going to do about this?'" She suggested that Jane try doing some of the things children do during play, like dancing, jumping around and throwing things in the air. Jane did as Kathy said, robotically jumping up and down, although it produced no change in Fluffy. But Jane was determined to make her dog happy somehow. She knew jokes made people happy, and although she couldn't tell jokes, she could now at least read. "So she read joke books to us," says Kathy. "It was very painful. We dutifully laughed at her jokes and they started getting better—but they were still pretty bad."

"One day we were watching her, jumping and hopping around in the field," says Kathy. "You could tell she'd been watching other people. Suddenly the dog started jumping and wagging his tail. We were so happy, we were all crying, and I don't know who we were happier for." In trying to make Fluffy happy, Jane had learned something important about her own happiness. Both Jane and Fluffy were transformed. Eventually, Fluffy found a permanent home. Jane was released from prison, got into a halfway house, found work and later moved into a group home. The woman no one ever expected to leave Kingston Penitentiary found untapped resources in herself. For Jane, one little dog made the difference.

Despite such successes, controversy continued to surround Canine Corrections. When Lakeside was closed, the program moved to the newer Burnaby Correctional Centre for Women, but its problems came along too. "We had a constant battle about this program," says Kathy. "I never got the financial support to develop the program along the lines I wanted." Detractors always questioned the purpose of the program and what it was actually accomplishing. Were these women all going to be dog trainers when they got out of prison? Over and over Kathy explained that, yes, the women learned a bit about dog training, but the true value was in the life skills they gained. "You never get a chance to practise all the things you learn in jail, like anger management, because you can't ever let your guard down. You've still got to protect yourself. But with the dogs," Kathy comments, "you get to use these skills."

Learning to be patient, open and vulnerable were huge steps. Most of the women seemed to understand that the dogs, like them, lived with tremendous pain and fear. "Learning to build relationships is a life skill, whether you learn it with a dog, a cat, a gerbil or a human," says Kathy. "The women quickly learned that they couldn't be frustrated or angry with the dogs." One might expect that women with violent pasts might be at risk for harming the dogs, but during the eight years that Kathy ran Canine Corrections, the worst thing that ever happened was when one inmate lost her temper, yelled at her dog and yanked on the leash. "This woman was so mortified, she called me right away and said, 'I have to tell you what I've done.' She voluntarily took herself out of the program." After dealing with the incident, the woman re-entered the program with a better understanding of herself. She'd learned the most valuable lesson of all: to recognize inappropriate behaviour in herself and to get help. After that, if she felt herself becoming frustrated, she stopped, gave the dog a break and called for help.

The inmates became very protective of their dogs and the program. Even in a crisis, their first thought was to keep their dogs safe. During the time Canine Corrections was in operation, an escape of inmates not involved in the program occurred. The area they escaped from was a blind spot near the kennel. "All the inmates knew what was going on," says Kathy, "even though no one could say anything." Without forethought, the kennel could have been damaged; dogs could have been frightened or hurt. However important the escape plan was to a few women, protecting the dogs was more important to them all. "The women made sure, even during the lockdown afterwards, that their dogs were okay."

Kathy's own Doberman, Eden, helped the inmates learn this kind of protectiveness. An amazing dog outside the institution, Eden had received numerous awards for her work in animal-assisted therapy and pet visitation. At Canine Corrections, she was the "practice dog."

"Eden literally trained the inmates," says Kathy. "If they made a mistake, she'd stop and give them hints about what they were supposed to do." And Eden's intuition wasn't restricted to the women in the program. One day, while Kathy was in a meeting, Eden got up, left her side and walked out of the room. Surprised, Kathy followed her. Eden had walked over to a cell down the hall, one that was often used to house new prisoners. The emotional residue of dozens of frightened women permeated the walls; it was a cell where bad things happened. When Kathy reached Eden's side, she looked into the cell. The woman inside was trying to hang herself. They'd just reached her in time. "Eden knew something was happening," Kathy says.

One day the Burnaby SPCA contacted Kathy about a shepherd-cross dog named Luke. He'd been running loose in the area for months, not vicious, but almost totally wild. In spite of his panicky demeanour, they'd finally managed to bring him in. Shelter workers told her no one could do anything with him, but Kathy decided to take him into Canine Corrections and see if the women could reach him. Kathy remembers, "When we went to get him he was standing frozen in the back of the kennel, absolutely terrified." At the prison, they put him in a quiet room where he'd be warm and dry, made sure he had food and water and left him alone.

Kathy paired Luke with Therese, a woman who'd been caught transporting drugs from Texas. Although she could have been sent to an institution closer to Texas in exchange for information, she wouldn't cut a deal for fear of retribution against her family down south. "She was trapped," says Kathy. "Neither Therese nor Luke really belonged there."

It took Luke several long weeks to settle in. Patiently, Therese began going into the room and just sitting on the floor with him. At first he flattened himself against the back wall, as far from her as he could get, terrified of what she might do to him. But she did nothing. Three times a day, she simply sat on the floor with him for awhile and then left.

Therese began trying to engage Luke with small treats. Although his ears came up and he looked at her outstretched hand with longing, he didn't have the courage to reach out to her. Then Therese discovered his weakness: peanut butter.

"All of the inmates started saving their peanut butter for Luke," says Kathy. "Finally the day came when Luke licked Therese's finger."

Therese decided Luke was ready to try a bit of freedom. "We put him on a long line and let him out to run. He ran and ran, with such joy!" says Kathy. "Except when he saw people. He was so scared of people." But each time he began to panic, Therese sat with him until he calmed down.

Luke developed another special friend in the program, a beagle-cross named Moxie. A well-mannered but head-strong little dog, Moxie took it upon herself to teach the other dogs some lessons in proper behaviour. The usual procedure when working with dogs like Luke was to let them out in the yard on a long line, allowing them the freedom to run while still having the means to catch them. "Moxie decided she'd teach Luke to walk on a loose line," explains Kathy. "She'd pick up his rope when she was walking outside with him. Whenever his leash got tight, she'd go in the opposite direction. She did this for a lot of dogs; she was a better trainer than most humans!" Before long, Luke took cues from Moxie for everything. If they wanted Luke to try something, they showed it to Moxie first. If she did it, he'd try it too.

"Luke got to a stage when he needed to go into a home," Kathy says. "Like the women, the dogs can only make so much progress inside the institution." But by this time it was apparent that Moxie and Luke couldn't be separated. Finally, after much searching, interviewing and preparation, they found a wonderful home willing to adopt the dogs together. Although Luke and Moxie have since passed away, people in the neighbourhood still talk about them. "Everyone loved them," says Kathy. "He and Moxie were a team."

When he and Moxie left Canine Corrections for their new home, Luke bore almost no resemblance to the trembling mass of insecurities he had been when he entered it. "There's no way anyone could have taken him on the way he was before," says Kathy. "We were able to create such a steady, stable atmosphere for these dogs that they became able to recover." In the process, many inmates were given the opportunity to recover from their own issues.

Year by year, in spite of opposition, the program evolved and grew. "It was a little piece of heaven," Kathy says. "It allowed me to experiment with everything I knew about dogs. I swear I learned as much as they did." Not only that, but the program was rehabilitating many dogs that would never have found homes otherwise. The "jailhouse dogs" developed a reputation; people went on waiting lists to get one of them. "People from all over wanted our dogs," says Kathy. "We sold them for a good price, even though they were basically mongrels." Charging for the dogs allowed the program to cover its costs, but nothing more.

Placing the dogs in homes gave the women in the program their final exam: to say goodbye. It was a tough assignment. These women had done all the hard work of helping these dogs become stable, socially appropriate citizens, able to find their place in the world. "For some of these women, Canine Corrections was the first success in their lives," says Kathy. "They'd done the work. And it earned them the right to approve or disapprove of the adoptive home. I had the final authority, but decisions were made as a group; we worked on it together."

Placing their dogs with families in the community gave program participants an unexpected bonus: it gave them a chance to interact with outsiders on an equal footing. They were able to see themselves—and be seen—not as prisoners, but as people. "They were an amazing bunch of women," Kathy says. "There was good and bad in all of them. I often told them that they were just like really smart, really rotten dogs, and if they'd ever gotten their brains focused in the right direction, they could have been millionaires!"

In 1998, the administrative powers fighting against the program finally prevailed, and Canine Corrections was discontinued. Although Kathy was devastated by the decision, she wasn't surprised. They were breaking ground for future programs in other institutions; the full value of their work would be recognized only in hindsight. It remains a highlight of her career, and the education she received from both the dogs and the inmates will never be forgotten. "I loved the prison program!" Kathy says. "Everyone won. The dogs won, the inmates won, the institution won and the community won."

2

Polly the Railroad Dog

ABOUT NINE YEARS AGO, a man named Tim Sundstrom went against the current. When everyone around him was moving into urban centres, he left the city and returned to Searchmont, Ontario, to live on the homestead where he'd been raised. He'd fought and won a battle against cancer, but lost his marriage of 16 years. The hunting and fishing he once enjoyed no longer appealed to him. His life had changed, and he needed a safe place in which to heal.

In the summer of 1997, the talk around town kept coming back to a little black dog that had been travelling for the last few weeks along the railroad tracks that cross through Searchmont. Tim's sister and brother-in-law, Irene and Bill Whyte, lived just outside Searchmont near the railway tracks. Long-time dog lovers, they were two of the first people to see her. According to rumour, the dog's original family had driven out from Sault Ste. Marie, opened their car door and dumped her out. "A friend of mine knew the dog and the owners who had abandoned her," says Tim. "He said he thought her name was Polly, and the dog did seem to know it." He added that he hoped he'd never meet the man who could do a thing like this to such a sweet dog.

The days shortened, the weather began turning crisp, and the residents began to worry about Polly. "She was very scruffy looking," says Tim. "People were setting food out, trying to catch her." But the little dog, which appeared to be a mix of border collie and spaniel, did not trust people. Like a ghost, she slipped from one shadow to another, stopping just long enough to bolt the scraps before disappearing again. If someone did manage to get close to her, she cowered in terror.

People even tried various tricks to catch her, but Polly refused to let herself be taken. "You can't help but be affected when you see something struggling to survive," says Tim. "People are good, and they meant well, but it probably scared her more than anything."

Tim suspected she was sleeping in a corner of the abandoned mill, which would at least provide shelter from the elements once winter set in. He and many others continued putting out food for her, but they wished they could get near enough to do more. She gratefully accepted whatever was set out for her.

Polly began to visit Tim's place regularly, trotting down his 45-metre driveway, sometimes even getting within arm's reach of him. One day he noticed with alarm that a collar was buried in the thick ruff around her neck. "I thought it was choking her, which really upset me," he says. But he knew better than to approach her. If he was going to help her at all, he first had to earn her trust.

He was sitting at the picnic table in his backyard one morning when Polly arrived, and this time she actually brushed up against him. When she looked at him, he saw the desperation in her gentle eyes, and he sensed that she'd made a decision. He slowly reached toward her, until he got one finger beneath the collar. It must have been put on her before she'd been fully grown, for it now constricted her neck. "I got a pair of scissors and off came the collar," says Tim. "If it had gotten wet and shrunk, it wouldn't have been a good thing." In their brief contact, Tim felt dense mats in her fur. But as soon as she was free of the collar, Polly darted away again.

But, working up her courage, each day she returned. "I left the screen door open in the evening," says Tim. "She'd just stay between the house and the creek at the back." Then one day, she darted in through the open door. She leaped over the threshold so fast and so fearfully that it looked to Tim as though she expected to be kicked. Afraid to spook her, Tim left the door open so she could go back and forth until she was comfortable. "The first night she stayed outside, but she kept coming back in," he says. "I figured that if she was going to stay, she'd stay. I'd let her decide." The next day he closed the door so she could stay inside. "She's been with me ever since," he says. The two of them began to heal each other.

Polly had decided to trust Tim, but would she ever become brave enough to interact with strangers? When company came to visit, Polly would disappear, hiding behind furniture or under beds. No amount of coaxing on the company's part could convince Polly to let people touch or come near her.

Then Tim met Lynne Pyette, a woman from his work who lived in Sault Ste. Marie. They became friends, but more importantly, so did their dogs. Lynne's Labrador retriever brought out something special in Polly. The other dog's calm, cheerful demeanour seemed to encourage her. "Polly seemed to really like my Lab, Misha," says Lynne, "and she learned to trust me as well."

"Polly's personality is really different from the skittish, untrusting, cautious nature she had at first," says Tim. "She gradually changed and now she won't hesitate to come out and mingle with people."

She'd learned that she was safe at Tim's house and safe with Tim's friends. But the memory of being left alone in a strange place never left her. Before going out of town a few months later, Tim took Polly to stay with his sister Irene, near the place where people thought Polly had been abandoned. "Polly knows them all really well, but it didn't matter, she wasn't going to stay there," Tim recalls. They let her outside to play with their two dogs. Within minutes, she scrambled through the fence and began walking down the train tracks, back to Searchmont. "Sure enough," says Tim, "Bill drove down the road looking for her, and when he got to Searchmont, there she was, just coming up to the crossing." She willingly got back in the truck with Bill and stayed near him and Irene until Tim returned for her. She was visibly relieved, however, when Tim returned to take her home. "I don't know how long dogs remember the terrible things that happen to them," he says, speaking of Polly's abandonment and her subsequent panic and starvation, "but hopefully those bad memories are pretty much gone."

Because Tim's sister Irene suffered chronic health problems, he went over frequently to visit and help out. Often, when he arrived, he was greeted by Charlie, a large Labrador–St. Bernard-cross. Charlie belonged to some people who lived in the same complex as Irene and Bill, people who did not appear responsible enough to care for themselves, let alone a dog. Charlie had grown accustomed to receiving handouts from Bill. "He wasn't getting fed very well," says Tim. "His eyes were sunken most of the time, and he looked underweight."

Irene heard rumours that Charlie's owners were planning to get rid of him. "Tell me if you are," she told them, "and I'll try and find him a home." She wasn't well enough to adopt Charlie herself, but neither she nor Bill could stand by

Charlie found a home with Polly and her owner

and do nothing. Her chances of finding a home for a large, old dog, though slim, were better than those he'd face at the pound. But Charlie's owners ignored her.

"One day, Irene called me at work," said Tim. "She told me, 'Charlie's gone. I think he's at the pound.' Lynne and I went down to the pound and sure enough, there he was in the cage, looking pretty forlorn." Charlie came home with Tim that day. "Every time Irene and Bill came out to Searchmont, Charlie would right away go over to Bill, who'd fed him when his owners wouldn't."

It takes a courageous heart to love in the face of imminent

loss. Not only was Polly in her twilight years, but now Tim had another old dog. His sister's health continued to worsen as well, and then doctors discovered that Bill had developed an aneurysm and needed surgery.

"This fall, Irene passed away," says Tim. "She'd been sick for 10 years, so it wasn't a surprise." But within three weeks of her death, Bill passed away suddenly. His aneurysm had ruptured before surgeons had a chance to repair it. "Who knows why these things happen?" Tim says.

Perhaps there is no reason, except to encourage us to take every opportunity to celebrate life and extend compassion wherever it is needed. "I used to be a hunter and now I'm a conservationist. I tell my little nieces and nephews that every living creature has a purpose." He laughs, then adds apologetically, "I even put spiders back outside, rather than kill them!"

Tim and Polly and Charlie will take whatever time they have and live it to the fullest. The timid little dog that once feared everyone now fiercely guards the boundaries of their property. "It doesn't matter the size of the dog," says Tim, "she's going to control the situation. Polly, with her border collie attitude—she's going to rule the roost!"

3

"Large Dog Needs Good Home"

IN JANUARY 2005, AN URGENT plea came from the Inuvik SPCA, at the point of the map where the Northwest Territories meets the Yukon. Could someone help a St. Bernard who needed to get "down" out of Inuvik? Because giant-breed dogs are difficult to house, many shelters, especially those in small communities, prefer to place them in foster homes or transfer them to breed-specific rescue groups. Inuvik had no place willing or able to take a young, untrained, 70-kilogram dog, and there are no breed-specific rescue groups in the area.

Fortunately, the e-mail went across Canada to Krys Prichard, dog-placement coordinator for Trinity of Hope Dog Rescue, headquartered in Manotick, Ontario. Trinity of Hope Dog Rescue is an organization committed to re-homing abandoned or unwanted giant breeds, especially St. Bernards and Newfoundlands. "The rescue community is small, and we were able to network with our representative in Edmonton," says Krys. "But my first thought was, 'Oh my God, Inuvik! Let me get a map.'"

Krys had arranged many such rescues, and she knew there was much to be done before they'd even know if this dog would make a suitable pet. "Most of them need between five and seven hundred dollars' worth of veterinary care before they're ready to be placed, and that's with the rescue discount," she explains. "They need to be thyroid-tested, they need treatment for parasites, they need vaccines, they need to be spayed or neutered and sometimes they need eye surgery."

But when Krys learned the history of this dog, named Ruby, she knew they would do everything they could to help her. Ruby's original owners, who lived in Inuvik, had purchased her from a breeder in the Edmonton area. Within the year, their family situation had changed and they no longer wanted her. They gave her away to a family who quickly lost interest in her as well. Ruby spent most of her time chained outside in the backyard, and when winter hit, she was in trouble. A good Samaritan felt sorry for the dog and offered to pay $100 for her. The second owners agreed, but when the new owner went to get her, he found things were worse than he'd thought; all but one foot of her chain had frozen to the ground. He literally had to chisel her out of the ice. "She was an 18-month-old puppy," notes Krys. "The breed standard states that females should be about 60 centimetres at the shoulder. With only 30 centimetres of free chain, this dog couldn't do anything but lie down."

The first hurdle was the more than 3,000 kilometres between Inuvik and Edmonton. Over the next three weeks, telephone calls and e-mails flew from one person to another, looking for a way to get this dog back to civilization. "We knew it would cost $1,200 for shipping alone, to get her out of the north," says Krys. A registered charity, Trinity of Hope is supported by community members and philanthropists, but this would severely tax their resources. Then they got the return phone call that changed everything. "Canadian North Airlines contacted us," says Krys. "The president of the airline himself called and said, 'Yes, we can do this for you.' That donation of the flight saved Ruby's life." And they didn't just stuff her crate into the cargo hold; they brought her out in style. Ruby and her giant dog kennel rode the entire way in the seat of honour, right behind the pilot. They even donated a seat for a volunteer to accompany her.

Krys knew they had to do something to express their appreciation. "We named her Trinity of Hope's Canadian North Gem," says Krys. "Our Miss Ruby." When Air Canada donated a flight to rescue a dog from Gander, Newfoundland, they named him Air Canada's Tanner Brown. WestJet has also expressed their willingness to help, and it's only a matter of time until they have a dog named after them as well. "We are very humbled by the support we receive in the community to help these big guys," Krys said.

"Our Edmonton representative spent countless hours getting Ruby ready to be adopted. He got her into a foster home, made sure she got cleaned up and dewormed, switched her from raw blubber to a proper diet, vaccinated and spayed her, had her dewclaws removed and had a microchip implanted. All this while running his own business and taking care of his parents. A true saint," Krys explained.

Finally, Ruby was ready to meet her new family. "All our homes are approved on a trial basis," says Krys. "They aren't just given a dog and then left on their own." Ruby went to a retired couple who were prepared for the demands of a giant breed and now, at two years of age, she is the light of their lives. She's finally getting the training, care and love she needs to blossom. "She went from being totally ignored, without much human contact at all, to being the centre of attention," says Krys.

Ruby's case ended well, but Krys worries about all the other dogs she hasn't heard of yet, especially those in remote locations. "Breeders should not be selling dogs to people who live in places like Inuvik," she says. "There are no veterinarians up there; they might have one that comes in three or four times a year, but if something happens to the dogs in between, the people take them out and shoot them."

Krys says the onus is on breeders to properly screen

buyers and prepare them for life with a large-breed dog. St. Bernard breeders often sell puppies without emphasizing that they need to be family dogs, not outdoor dogs. Inexperienced owners love the puppy, but are unprepared for an energetic adolescent dog that may outweigh them. "The St. Bernard puppy gets to be 18 months old and very big," Krys says. "He's untrained, roaming and barking, so he gets dumped."

Most purebred dog fanciers are very protective of their breeds. The best breeders require puppy buyers to sign an agreement stating that, if they are unable to keep the dog for any reason, at any time in the future, they will return it to the breeder. Such breeders often participate in breed-specific rescue and foster programs. Part of Trinity of Hope's mandate is to work with these purebred-dog rescue groups, getting the biggest of them out of municipal shelters and into appropriate foster homes. This allows the shelters to focus their resources on the mixed-breed dogs that have no such groups to advocate for them.

"We focus on big dogs, because that's what we have," says Krys. "When the Ottawa Humane Society became rescue-friendly in 1998, I went to them and asked, 'What can we do to help you?' My husband and I had Newfs at the time, and I knew that giants are difficult because they don't do well in shelters."

So Krys contacted the breed rescue groups whenever a purebred dog came into the shelter. Then she helped get the dogs out of the shelter and into the safety of the breed rescue group. "Between 2000 and 2001 I transported 176 purebred dogs from the humane society to breed rescue groups located in various places." She didn't restrict herself to large-breed dogs at the time; everything from shelties, corgies and collies to labs and boxers were scooped and sent to safe havens.

Although Krys and her husband began doing giant-breed rescue in 1993, it wasn't until 1998 that an abandoned Rottweiler named Hope galvanized Krys into creating an "official" rescue group. "The Rottweiler was sedated, all ready for euthanasia, when they called us," remembers Krys. "I couldn't take her myself, because I had dogs that were being kept quarantined, awaiting international health certificates. So I called around until I got a foster home. Three of us ended up working together, so we called ourselves Trinity of Hope."

Their mandate is to keep an eye out for Newfoundland and St. Bernard dogs that end up in shelters. They also provide assistance for groups transporting dogs from one location to another. Trinity of Hope's biggest strength is the network of committed dog lovers supporting them. One year, Krys was contacted about a dog that needed to be relocated from Edmonton to Winnipeg. "We had a volunteer who drove half of the way—about 11 hours from Edmonton," says Krys. "Another volunteer from Winnipeg drove out to meet him. That's pretty good commitment."

But Krys and her like-minded dog lovers also do a form of crisis intervention, in an attempt to keep dogs in homes that might otherwise be forced to give them up. "It's called a bailment agreement," says Krys. "That means that the person still owns the property, but someone else is using it or caring for it." Most of the time, these dogs are temporarily displaced during the disruption of divorce. Sometimes the crisis is due to domestic violence, where the woman needs a secure place for her dog while she is in a safe house. One time they took care of a dog while the owner was undergoing treatment for breast cancer. "We do this on a case-by-case basis, and it all depends on whether or not there's someone willing to do it," she says. "There can be some risk to the people doing the work, especially in the case of domestic violence, so we have to make sure the person who's harbouring the animal isn't at risk. We'd like this to be a nationwide program, but it is limited to what we can do."

Today Krys has five dogs of her own as well as two foster dogs, all Newfoundlands or St. Bernards. Almost 450 kilograms of dog is a bit much, even for her, but she knows these dogs have no other place to go. "My own are all unadoptable for various reasons. I've got a fenced yard and no children, so I'm able to keep them fairly easily and keep them safe." But there are never enough experienced volunteers to go around, and when the dogs end up at Krys' door, she can't turn them away. "Fate always intervenes," she adds, "and they do find homes, even better homes than ours. It just takes time. We don't euthanize dogs just because they've been here too long. We know their families are out there somewhere."

Every dog has a story, and it takes patience to find that

perfect ending. "All of them are pathetic in the sense that the people who committed to them threw them away," she says. "Every dog is special."

But one dog has become something more than special to her: an 11-year-old male named Captain Kirk S. Bernard, ret. L.O. (retired Lawn Ornament). Krys remembers her introduction to this special canine.

"In 1999 I was told about a 'tricoloured Newfoundland' that was in the humane society and needed help," she says. She'd been rescuing large- and giant-breed dogs for several years at that point, and had recently established Trinity of Hope. Although St. Bernards weren't very common, the shelter often called her about Newfoundlands. Krys knew very well that Newfs are black or, very rarely, black and white, but never tricoloured. "I hadn't seen a St. Bernard for about 20 years then, but I knew that's what this was," she says. He'd been relinquished to the shelter in the aftermath of a divorce. No one had the time or inclination to care for him; he was tied to a tree during the day and put in the garage at night. "He knew nothing," says Krys. "I call him my 'I know nuthin' dog.'"

"The minute I saw him," she remembers, "he rolled over for me to scratch his belly, and I fell in love." Krys took him home and began her usual routine of phoning around for the nearest rescue group dealing with this breed. That's when she learned that, in all of Canada, there was not a single St. Bernard rescue organization. "It really broke our hearts to hear that they had no help, and that so many were so poorly treated," she says.

She refused to take him back to the shelter, because all the "rescue-friendly" staff members were away on summer holidays. "I was a little nervous to leave him there because his euthanasia fee had already been paid," she says. So she brought him home and began arranging for his medical care. Kirk, she discovered, would not make it easy on her; not only was he suffering from a severe kidney infection, but he tested positive for heartworm, a potentially deadly mosquito-borne parasite. Fortunately, once word got out, donations began flowing in. The Saint Bernard Club of America, a Saint Rescue group in Minnesota and Drs. Kim and Richard Smith all helped with medical expenses.

Krys explains the dog's unusual name. He had actually been named Curt by his original family, but Krys misunderstood it as "Kirk." "The first day he came home with me, he hadn't had any vaccines yet, so I wanted to keep him apart from my other dogs," she says. "I set up a stall for him in the barn, with water, a sleeping bag and some toys. I closed the tack room, closed the barn and came inside and went to bed."

Her husband had gone out that night and she wasn't expecting him home until the wee hours. "When he came home at 1:00 a.m., he asked me why I'd left the St. Bernard out in the yard. I told him I hadn't! 'Well,' he said, 'I guess it must be another St. Bernard outside in the yard.' Since this was the first one I'd seen in 20 years, I figured that wasn't very likely." When she insisted that she'd safely locked up their new dog, he responded, "So what happened? Did he get beamed up?"

"We went to look and found that he'd eaten a hole in the barn." Krys smiles at the memory, adding, "If a Saint wants to get out, he gets out!" But the dog's name was Captain Kirk from that moment on.

Their handsome new dog quickly worked his way into their household and their hearts. It was as if he'd always lived with them. Then one evening, at the age of five, Captain Kirk got sick. It was evening and he'd been asleep, but when he went outside last thing at night, something suddenly went very wrong. Within a matter of seconds, his belly looked like a 55-gallon drum. Krys' husband yelled, "Kirk's bloating." Krys immediately called her friend and veterinarian, Dr. J. Within seven minutes Dr. J. and her husband met Krys and her husband at the clinic.

Kirk was experiencing one of the biggest health problems of large-breed dogs: gastric dilation-volvulus, also known as "bloat" or "twisted stomach." The name says it all. This condition occurs when the stomach twists on its axis, trapping gas and food inside. The pressure builds until the blood supply to the stomach is compromised. It's a critical emergency that requires immediate intervention; even then, many dogs do not survive.

"When the surgeon opened him up and saw the purple

necrotic tissue inside, he said, 'This dog's a dead dog, you gotta make the call,'" remembers Krys. "I looked at my husband, read his eyes and told the surgeon, 'The goalie's out. Go for broke. Unless he dies, you keep working.'" Krys remembers holding her hand in front of Kirk's nose throughout the operation.

That was six years ago, and the same veterinarian has worked on Kirk many more times since then. Today, at 11 years of age, Kirk has long outlived his statistical lifespan. "He's definitely my cottage mortgage," Krys admits wryly. "I'd rather have him than the cottage. He makes us laugh every day, and he's very, very handsome. Must have been the cutest puppy in the world. How could anybody have just tied him up and thrown him away?"

4

Black Dogs

THE FIRST DOG I REALLY remember was Fluffy, a black spaniel-cross. We got her when I was about eight years old. My parents had bought country property on which stood an ancient two-room schoolhouse that they gutted and moved onto a new basement. Fluffy lived outside most of the time, but in the pit of Saskatchewan winter, she was allowed to sleep in the porch. We had cats, geese, chickens and even, for one summer, a mare and her foal. Fluffy had a couple of litters of puppies, sired by nondescript mongrels that appeared out of nowhere and given away amidst copious tears on my part.

As much as possible, I lived outdoors during the summer, revelling in the music of the meadowlarks, the splash of sunset on golden fields, the ripple of wind over acres of ripe grain. Willow bushes bent their limbs over hidden, moss-covered pathways. Tiny frogs jumped amongst the tough slough grasses, easily evading our clumsy hands. Cattails waved in the wind; in the fall, we split open their brown heads, blowing clouds of seeds into the sky.

Two years later we moved back to the city. Looking back, I understand my parents' decision, but it was a dreadful time for me. I had to leave behind my old friends and make new ones, which I always found to be an ordeal. My wide-open playground shrunk to a small city lot with houses on each side and a road in front. Most of the animals couldn't come with us, but, thankfully, we didn't leave Fluffy behind.

The kids at my new school eyed me with suspicion, a naïve hayseed who didn't wear the right clothes or understand their slang or their games. These girls were harder, older, with an edge I couldn't contend with. They liked clothes, boys and makeup and certainly weren't interested in animals or reading. Many nights I cried myself to sleep, dreading the next school day. I grew taller, thinner and quieter, my only ambition to become invisible.

I wouldn't know it for many years, but the environment in which I found myself was copiously fertilizing the seeds of depression sown in my DNA and nurtured by my introspective personality. All I knew at the time was that I was impossibly shy. I never raised my hand in class, although every time someone else volunteered the answer I was secretly whispering, I kicked myself inside. I avoided schoolyard games wherever possible, certain my teammates would only yell at me for making mistakes. At church socials, kind-hearted women who urged me to "Smile!" and "Say something!" were unaware that their words only made me squirm in humiliation.

A few years later, to my immense relief, we moved back to the country. Fluffy had space to run again and quickly memorized the boundaries of our new, larger property. I'd managed to make a few friends in the city, but none of them could make me want to stay. Even the thought of starting over at a new school couldn't entirely dampen my enthusiasm.

My first week in grade eight, I met Kathi, who lived on a neighbouring farm and loved animals the same way I did. One day after school, I learned that her dad had brought home a tiny, cream-coloured puppy named Tippy. But there was a problem. Their resident Airedale hated Tippy on sight. From the moment the new puppy set foot on their yard, there had been no peace. Tippy would have to go. Did I want him?

When I walked up the driveway, the puppy nestled in my arms, my parents knew they couldn't refuse me. Suddenly I had a dog of my very own! And not the usual large, dark, shaggy farm dog. Tippy was small, with smooth, short, tan-coloured fur and golden-tipped ears and tail. Only his nose and eyes were black.

I set about becoming the best dog owner I could be. I borrowed library books about dog training. I read about grooming and shows and dog food. He was just an unwanted, crossbred pup, but I was determined to make him as good as any pedigreed dog. Without any formal guidance the two of us muddled through as best we could, and although we were never going to win any prizes, Tippy and I formed a powerful bond. Unlike Fluffy, who was allowed onto the porch if she was lucky, Tippy got to sleep in my room, on the foot of my bed, and there was no doubt about it—he loved me with his whole heart.

Tippy's loyalty was rock solid. During my high-school years, I was plagued by recurrent streptococcus infections. Each winter, like clockwork, I lost a week of school, sick in bed with my throat on fire. At these times, Tippy never left my side. My mother came in regularly with chicken soup, mentholated ointment and fresh sheets. Tippy watched her from the foot of my bed while she felt my forehead and listened to my raspy voice. If I was asleep when she came in, however, Tippy got up and stood between us. He didn't threaten my mother, exactly, but he made it clear that no one would touch me without permission. It was his job to watch over me.

During the summers we rambled over the back pasture, me with my head in the clouds, Tippy and Fluffy chasing jackrabbits and gophers. I taught Tippy to climb ladders, and on warm summer evenings he and I often sat together in the treehouse. He never learned to climb down, however, and howled frantically until I gave in and carried him down.

One day a strange dog wandered onto our property while Tippy and I were down at the dugout. The large, black dog didn't appear menacing, but neither did he appear friendly. I didn't know what to do, so I just stood still, hoping he would go home. Tippy, however, went ballistic. He barked and barked, running circles around the trespasser, slowly edging him away from me. Eventually the dog decided that whatever he'd been after wasn't worth the trouble, and he left. Tippy pranced back to me proudly, as if his 11 kilograms of bravado had done the trick.

After high school, I was away from home during the academic year in order to pursue my education. One summer I came home to the news that Tippy had been killed by a car on the highway. His body was already gone. In tears, I combed the ditches near where he had been struck, hoping to find his collar so I would have something tangible to remember him by. I found nothing. My little friend was gone for good. It would be 20 years before I was ready to risk my heart as a dog owner again.

A lifetime later, when I told my husband, Ray, that I wanted a puppy for my birthday, my decision wasn't made lightly. We had kids and the routine of a busy family life. We had cats. We had birds. And we already had one dog, a greyhound called Molly. But although Molly expected me to feed her and clean up after her, she'd attached herself heart and soul to Ray.

For years I'd fallen into bed exhausted, following days filled with diapers, high chairs and car seats. I'd gestated and lactated, survived postpartum depression and gone for years at a time without a full night's sleep. I'd fed and clothed three small bodies, challenged three small minds and guided three small hearts that needed my encouraging wisdom. I was Mother. Hear me roar.

But the whirlwind stage had passed, leaving me in the dust. My three daughters could now feed and clothe themselves. They challenged me as much as I challenged them. And they smiled indulgently at my motherly "wisdom."

I'd worked hard to be a good mother—and I'd worked myself out of a job. It begged the question: if I was no longer necessary in the role I'd become so good at, who was I? I'd long since lost the skills necessary for the job I had "Before Children." The writing career I'd developed had reached a yawning plateau I seemed unable to leap across. I was no longer passionate about writing ad copy for pet food, and if I had to craft one more clever, scintillating article about getting rid of fleas, I was going to lose what remained of my mind. I wanted to write *stories*. But no one, it seemed, was interested in reading them, much less publishing them or paying me for them. I was floundering, and it scared me. With my 40th birthday approaching, I wondered if this was that much-maligned cliché, the mid-life crisis. In the wee hours, plagued by restlessness, I felt the black dogs of depression nipping at my heels.

Yes, a puppy would distract me. Years previously, at a dog show, I'd seen an agility demonstration. From the first moment, I knew that one day I wanted to do that with my own dog. For agility, I knew I needed a smart, athletic dog. Many different breeds excelled at agility, but the fastest, most impressive dogs I'd seen were all border collies. I decided I wanted a border collie.

"Oh, no, you don't," said Ray. In his veterinary practice, he treats many kinds of dogs every day, often when they're sick or in pain. If there's a worst-case scenario, he's seen it. "They're way too intense. A border collie would drive you crazy."

So I suggested a Shetland sheepdog; they're beautiful, smart, and I love that rich sable colour.

"Too yappy," he said. "And way too hairy."

A Welsh springer spaniel? I'd seen one at the beach a few summers ago and was impressed by the tough, compact body and lovely red-and-white coat.

"Springer rage syndrome," he said. "Besides, they're pretty rare."

Nova Scotia duck toller? Ray rolled his eyes.

Australian shepherd? "Oh, please."

Now, let me be clear: my husband loves me, and he loves dogs. Most of his patients come to see him with their tails wagging, pulling their owners into the exam room, where the dogs know cookies are waiting. He loves meeting new puppies and caring for them as they grow up. He loves watching as the bond between people and their dogs grows year by year. But every day he hears a laundry list of the things that drive dog owners batty about their beloved pets. He knows the typical health and behaviour problems each breed is prone to and can predict which puppies will need ear medication, which ones will blow their knees and which ones will eat the linoleum. He also knows better than anyone how important it is to get a good "fit" between dog and owner.

One by one, we went through my favourite breeds. He had an argument against each one.

"Alright," I said finally. "Which breed do *you* think I should get?" It was the opening he'd been waiting for.

"A miniature poodle," he answered promptly.

A *poodle*? Was he serious? I was turning 40, not 70. Poodles were lapdogs, old-lady dogs, high-strung, neurotic, yappy dogs. I'd never even considered this breed.

"Trust me, a poodle is the perfect dog for you," he insisted.

By that time it was summer already, and I was ready to agree to anything. I began researching miniature poodles, locating people who raised them in our area. Before long, I grudgingly admitted he might just be right. Most of the poodles I'd previously seen were either tiny toy poodles or crossbred dogs such as cock-a-poos, malti-poos and Lhasa-poos. The wave of popularity that once did such damage to all three varieties of the breed—standard, miniature and toy—had long since moved on to other dogs.

Poodles are smart and very trainable, I read, and also athletic enough for the sports I wanted to try. And I had to admit that, with all the cat fur everywhere, a non-shedding dog might be an excellent choice for our home. I began to visualize my puppy. I wanted a cream-coloured one, like Tippy, or maybe apricot. Even white. Just not black. Black is boring, the default setting.

In August I met Doris, a breeder of beautiful miniature poodles, all show champions. She screened all her breeding stock for genetic diseases and raised only one or two litters each year, in her home. It was perfect! We went out to see her and meet her dogs. They were all lovely: two white females who'd already earned their championships, a gorgeous young male in full white show coat, and one black female named Nina, who came to meet us with a toy in her mouth. Guess which one was pregnant?

It would be a year or longer before any white puppies were available, so I filled out the application form and got my name on the list. But if all went well, the puppies from Doris' pregnant black poodle would be ready to go to their new homes right around my birthday in November. Karma like that couldn't be ignored, so I resigned myself. Not only was I getting a *poodle*, but I was getting a *black* one.

Over the next few weeks, as Nina grew larger, Doris sent numerous e-mails with photos attached: Nina with her ball, Nina in the whelping box, Nina surrounded by stuffed animals and squeaky toys. Even though black dogs don't photograph very well, the sparkle in her eye and her fun-loving nature shone through clearly.

The poodle lineup—five shiny black sausages

Then one day in early September 2003, my inbox showed a message with the subject line "Puppies!" The photos showed a tired-looking Nina with five shiny black sausages lined up against her abdomen. In a few weeks, Doris told us, we could visit them. In the meantime, she would send us regular updates on their development.

Then came the unexpected phone call that changed everything. It was my doctor, calling about some test results. "You've got a mass on your ovary," she said. "You need to see a specialist, and you'll have to have surgery." I was told to plan for full abdominal surgery—with six to eight weeks of recovery time!

"But, my puppy," I thought.

Then I thought, "My ovary."

When the gynecologist looked at my ultrasound report, he confirmed my doctor's assessment that yes, I needed surgery. "It's probably not cancer," he continued casually, picking up his calendar, "but we need to nail down the surgery date." I'm sure he meant it to be comforting, but my brain barely registered the "probably not" part, instead focusing directly on the "cancer" part. The operation was scheduled for the morning of Halloween. The Day of the Dead. More comforting thoughts.

The month that followed was one of the longest in my life. I'd been warned that the biggest concern was that the tumour, known as a cystic teratoma, could twist on its axis and rupture, causing internal bleeding, so I walked carefully, as though cradling a ticking time bomb in my belly.

"Squishy the Cyst," as we wryly referred to it, was growing daily inside me, reminding me constantly of its presence with a dull ache punctuated by occasional bursts of terrifying pain. The formerly free-floating anxiety of mid-life was now the least of my worries.

I quietly put my affairs in order—cleaned the bathrooms, paid all the bills and threw out all the underwear with holes in it. But I refused to give up my puppy. Doris kept sending photos. She'd picked out a sturdy male for me and given him a dot of nail polish on one toe to distinguish him from his brother. The last time we had gone to visit, he toddled eagerly after us, curious and interested. He was adorable, and I'd already picked out his name—Myshkin, after the Russian prince in Dostoevsky's *The Idiot*.

The morning of the surgery arrived. I kissed my husband

and each of my daughters, took a deep breath and tried to look brave and crusty like Debra Winger in the movie *Terms of Endearment*. After the lengthy form-filling, blood-letting, insertion of intravenous lines and telling 14 different people that no, I hadn't had anything to eat or drink since the night before, I walked through the doors to the surgery ward. Quaking with nerves and cold, I entered the frigid, ice-green surgical suite and climbed up gingerly onto the operating table, intravenous tubes trailing along. The operating room nurses and anaesthesia technicians bustled about, laying out instrument packs on the counters and fiddling with dials. The surgeon had decided the cyst couldn't be removed endoscopically, that is, without a surgical incision, so I would need general anaesthesia. The anaesthetist emptied a syringe filled with clear-coloured liquid into my IV line, and my world faded to black.

I awoke to see my husband's face floating dimly above me. "You did great, honey," he whispered, holding up the digital camera. "See?" On the tiny screen was an image of a gloved hand holding an ice-cream container with a shiny, wet-looking softball at the bottom.

"Bye-bye, Squishy," I slurred. Then he showed me a few shots of the girls in their Halloween costumes, ready to go off with their friends. But I was, already drifting back into an uneasy sleep, my anaesthetic-induced dreams filled with children dressed as butchers, holding severed organs.

One week later I was sitting in my writing room, feet up, my laptop on a pillow on my lap, a glass of water and a painkiller sitting at the ready. Ray had given me strict instructions to sit still and wait. He and the girls were bringing Myshkin home.

When they arrived, I hobbled outside to meet them. Ray opened the crate and let the puppy out onto the grass. The little fellow looked overwhelmed and frightened, but oh so cute! Doris had bathed and trimmed him and put little blue bows in his hair. Suddenly, my throat closed up. I knew just how he felt. Here he was, not knowing what lay ahead of him, unsure of where he belonged. Here I was, having faced my mortality for the first time and now looking at a new stage of life, unsure of what lay around the corner.

I gathered Myshkin in my arms, a little ball of fluff, and he settled down against me. Together, we would find out what came next.

CHAPTER

5

Hugs for Blaster

IN 1994, WHEN I WAS pregnant with our third child, we moved from our crowded townhouse into a spacious, detached split-level. The first thing I thought when the deal went through was that we'd finally be able to get a dog! But with two small children and another on the way, we decided that instead of a puppy we'd adopt an adult dog. Friends suggested we look at retired racing greyhounds, and within a few months Molly joined us. At two years old, Molly had been culled from the racing program because she was too small, barely bigger than an oversized whippet. An elegant, graceful dog, she ran like a dancer, with joy in every step. Her soft dark eyes begged us to be gentle with her; we loved her on sight.

We thought we were prepared, but we quickly learned that rescued greyhounds can come with a great deal of baggage. Molly wasn't house-trained. She ran away on us. She dug gigantic holes in the backyard. But the biggest problem was that when she got anxious, she peed. On the carpet, in her crate, on beds and couches. We nearly gave up on her, but every time we thought we couldn't take it anymore, we remembered what we loved about her. Anti-anxiety medication finally helped calm her fears and save our ravaged carpets.

Twelve years later, Molly is still with us. At 14, she's even thinner now, and suffering from advanced kidney disease. She's nearly blind and doesn't hear well anymore. But she still loves her daily romp outside and the cookie she gets when she comes in. We know she won't be with us much longer, but we've been through so much with her, we can't imagine life without her. Greyhounds, we've discovered, have a way of worming themselves into your heart.

We're not alone. Greyhound rescue groups have sprung up across North America in the past few decades, and more and more ex-racing dogs are finding their way into pet homes. And people like Judy and Jim Sleith of Calgary, Alberta, have discovered that greyhounds are like peanuts: it's hard to stop at one.

Jim and Judy are volunteers with Chinook Winds Greyhound Rescue Foundation in Calgary, Alberta. Chinook Winds is a non-profit organization dedicated to the rescue and adoption of retired racing greyhounds. "I've been doing this for five years," says Judy. "Last year we brought up about 12 dogs every four to six weeks. We rescued about 125 our first year and it's up to about 150 per year now." Although an executive of 4 runs the group, they have a province-wide network of 80 volunteers who help out.

Although no legislation exists to make professional greyhound racing illegal, the sport remains almost nonexistent in Canada. South of the border, however, it's another story. Dog racing is a popular spectator sport in more than a dozen US states, where gambling at the dog tracks is very similar to that at horse races. Also like horses, racing dogs are valuable commodities to their owners; most owners take the steps necessary to protect and nurture these assets.

In addition to state regulations they must follow, most racetracks have their own rules, policies and procedures to protect the well-being of the racers. In exchange for the right to run their greyhounds at a track, kennel owners are required to follow all track rules, including those pertaining to animal welfare. If kennel owners violate these rules, they risk losing not only their track privileges, but their racing licences as well. Unfortunately, since the Animal Welfare Act does not cover greyhound racing in the USA, these standards of care are regulated only by the industry itself.

Each year in America, approximately 34,000 greyhounds are born into the racing industry. They begin their lives on breeding farms, where they are raised and trained until the age of 18 months, at which time they are sent to a kennel where they begin preparing to race. Those with potential to make money for their owners are kept. Those that are slow, sick or injured are culled. When dogs retire from racing, usually by age five, they are used for breeding, are euthanized or are handed over to a rescue group. That's where groups like Chinook Winds come in.

"Our dogs usually come from one of five places: Arizona, Colorado, Oklahoma, Kansas or Wisconsin," says Judy.

In October 2005, a shipment of 15 greyhounds left their homes in Kansas, destined for new lives in far-off Alberta. Before they are allowed to come into Canada, all retired greyhounds must be "processed," or given a clean bill of health, so the dog hauler stopped in Coeur d'Alene, Idaho, where a veterinarian was waiting for them. There, each dog was examined and given the required vaccinations. Rescue people are accustomed to the routine, but this time something was different.

While most of the dogs are anxious while travelling, one big male named Acme Blasting was so afraid of people, he was nearly volcanic with terror. "They couldn't touch him anywhere, especially his hindquarters," recalls Judy. "He would just tuck his hips in and almost do back flips or hang himself to get away. He almost got away on them in Coeur d'Alene."

But they managed, and then it was time for the next leg of their journey, to Moyie Lake, where they were given a week to settle down. A Chinook Winds member used this time to observe the dogs and profile their personalities. "We almost always have people waiting in the wings for dogs to arrive, and we like to do some preliminary matching of the dogs to their adoptive families," explains Judy.

The next step was to bring the dogs to Calgary, where they would be placed into foster homes to await permanent adoption. Some dogs spent a few days in a boarding kennel while the details are sorted out. Members of the group visited the dogs, took them for walks and tried to get to know them a bit. Judy drove about 1,000 kilometres that week, going back and forth several times a day to walk the dogs. "That's where I met Blaster," says Judy. "I'd heard about how shy he was, but the first time I saw him, I thought, 'Oh, my God! What are we ever going to do with this boy?'"

In order to get a leash over his head, one person had to approach him from the front and one from the rear. He'd wriggle through the slightest opening, jumping and scrambling away in terror, always evading those dreaded human hands. But in his fear, his goal was always escape, not defence. Not once has Blaster threatened to bite.

The volunteer home Blaster was supposed to go to was fairly new to greyhound rescue, and Judy quickly realized this dog would require far more care than most. "When I heard how fearful he was, I knew there was no way he could go to an inexperienced foster home, so I said I'd take him."

For some people, one greyhound always leads to another. "It's true!" agrees Judy. "You can't possibly keep them all, but there's something special about each and every one of them."

Mature greyhounds can weigh 25 to 35 kilograms and mea-sure 75 centimetres at the shoulder. With three permanent greyhounds of their own, and usually a foster or two as well, Judy and Jim were used to "a lot of dog" around the home. "It's amazing," she says. "We often walk into the house and can't see even one of them. They're all sound asleep on a bed somewhere." Although these canine sprinters can run up to 70 kilometres an hour, between runs they love nothing better than a soft, warm couch to curl up on.

They'd also recently fostered several "special needs" grey-hounds with health and behavioural problems. Judy, a regis-tered nurse, is undaunted by even serious medical problems. She expected Blaster to get over his shyness quickly.

Blaster arrived in his new foster home on Wednesday, October 26, afraid of the world and everything in it. He'd never seen stairs before and had no idea how to go up or down them. Since no one could touch him, simply getting him in and out of the house was a challenge. Because track dogs are used to being surrounded by other greyhounds all the time, they're usually comfortable being fostered with other retired racers. They learn the routine by following the experienced dogs. Not Blaster.

Seven-year-old Sterling, a red-and-white male, had no interest in this skittish new dog. Six-year-old Firebolt, a white-and-black female, looked at him with suspicion. Only the oldest, 10-year-old Beth, a black brindle retired "brood mom," was willing to take him under her wing.

Blaster was overwhelmed. At the track, life revolves around a never-changing schedule. The dogs live indoors, in crates measuring one metre wide by just over a metre deep by slightly less than a metre high. The crates are usually stacked, with females on the upper level and males on the lower level. Four times a day, like clockwork, the dogs are "turned out" for exercise and an opportunity to relieve themselves. In many kennels, the dogs begin barking within minutes of the scheduled turnout time. They spend about 20 minutes running around in a fenced run, females with females, males with males. Then they go back into their crates.

Now, in a world of uncertainty, Blaster retreated to the only place he felt safe: his crate. But Judy wasn't daunted. "We could see in his eyes from the beginning that although his whole world had been turned upside down, he very much wanted to trust us," says Judy. "It was probably six weeks before I could get a leash on him to take him out of the yard. He was able to follow the other dogs out the open door, able to come and go as he pleased, but he pretty much lived in his crate."

Many retired racing greyhounds have issues with things they've never been exposed to, such as stairs, mirrors, linoleum flooring, children, cats and other animals. But these things weren't Blaster's big fear. "It was people that scared him," says Judy. "The other things he could cope with. I've dealt with a lot of shy dogs that get labelled spooks, but all those dogs find their comfort, when they finally come around, in humans. Not

Blaster. At that point he'd have been quite happy if there were no humans in his life. It was a pretty big project."

So, with Blaster, human contact was the first obstacle to overcome. They took it slowly. "Every time he walked by me, ran by me, I'd put my hand out and touch him," says Judy. "That's all we did." She turned it into a game. When Blaster allowed Judy to touch him, he got a cookie. Gradually, she built up his tolerance to the point where he would let her rub her hands over his body, even his touchy back end, in exchange for a treat.

Within a few weeks, they saw improvement. Although he still avoided body contact, he'd become more receptive to physical affection, even joining the other dogs when they ran up for hugs and treats. When Judy arrived home from work, Blaster met her at the door with excitement, his tail wagging wildly, ready to let her stroke him gently. He'd even begun to run to the door to meet Jim, who was nowhere near Judy in Blaster's opinion.

He also discovered the joys of home life. He learned that there were other beds besides the one in his crate, and some of them were big and really comfortable. He discovered stuffies and squeaky toys.

One morning, a month or so after he arrived, Blaster woke up in a particularly brave mood. "He ran all over the house, each time down the hallway with a different stuffie in his mouth, like he just couldn't get over this new world of toys," says Judy. He also began play-bowing, that canine invitation to a game of tag, shaking his head and barking. He began to come out of his shell.

Then it was time for a challenge. Blaster needed to be neutered, but how would he handle the hospital?

It was as if the previous few weeks hadn't even happened. At the clinic, he was terrified of being touched and had to be sedated for handling. When Judy went to pick him up after the surgery, the technician went to take him out of the crate without putting his leash on first. Big mistake! "He leaped out of the crate, up on the treatment room counter, sending everything flying. Then he jumped down again, dashed out of the room, off up a set of stairs, and into the vet's office, where he hid in a corner. We had a terrible time getting him out of there." Judy couldn't believe what she was seeing. It was like watching a car crash in slow motion. Where had all his progress gone?

She worried that without intervention Blaster might never overcome his fears. They brought in experts, animal behaviourists who evaluated Blaster and offered suggestions. "One suggested we take his crate away. This backfired on us. He was totally upset, bouncing off walls and just beside himself. He couldn't deal with the loss of his comfort zone. We probably knocked back his progress by three months."

So they took a few steps back, working once more on encouraging and supporting him in his attempt to learn trust and confidence again. They focused on exercises in confidence building, using clicker training. But it looked like it would take Blaster years to learn what another dog might master in weeks.

When their veterinarian suggested medication to help reduce Blaster's anxiety, Judy hoped this common solution would be what the dog needed, but he refused to do his part. "He had three days of it and he quit eating entirely because the pills were in his food," she says. "The one and only time I thought he might bite me was when I was trying to pill him. In the end, we were so stressed that we decided to continue on the way we'd been going and hope for the best."

After the pill incident, his eating habits, finicky to begin with, became extreme. They decided to try making his food issues work for them. The behaviourist suggested they switch him from kibble to a semi-moist diet he couldn't resist. All his food was to be fed to him by hand—and he had to work for each piece. The message for Blaster was this: nothing is free, and you have to trust us.

"He looked good and hadn't lost any weight, but it took energy and patience every day to get enough food into him. We'll probably always have food battles," says Judy. "He could still use a couple more pounds—he's a big dog."

"At some point I began to think he might not be adoptable," admits Judy. "He was fearful of absolutely everything, right down to his food. He would check out every ounce, every iota of food in his bowl before he ate it. I don't know what he thought he was going to find in there. It's painful to sit and watch him eat one piece at a time."

Judy never intended to adopt Blaster. "When I had one greyhound, I wasn't planning on adopting a second," she says with a smile. "When I had two, I wasn't planning on adopting a third. The second and third were my husband's decision." But one day, events occurred to change her mind. "We had a four-greyhound escape from our yard, and Blaster was one of the escapees," she recalls. "I was able to catch three of the four, but Blaster was gone. We live at a key intersection, but our house is the fourth house from the corner. Before I'd gotten one house away, I saw him. He just sat at the corner, his little ears down. I wondered how on earth I'd catch him. So I crouched down and called him, then ran back into the yard. He followed me through the gate! Then he did a perfect 'down.' He never does that! I told my husband, 'If he's so scared of the world that he wants to come home, then he has to stay here.'" The fact that Blaster had trusted her enough to come when she called him made Judy realize he already was home.

And that was that. One morning, as the light softly peeked in under her bedroom blinds, Judy stretched out her legs and bumped something heavy at the foot of her bed. She opened her eyes, lifted her head and gasped. Blaster, his warm, sleepy body nestled in the folds of the quilt, had tucked himself in between Judy and her husband.

Now, a year after his arrival, he is finally settling down. "Take him beyond the barriers of our fence and he becomes the same dog he was a year ago, fearful of everything," she says. "But when it's just me, or me and my husband and our dogs, in our own home, in our own yard, he acts like the two-year-old puppy he is. He has the most fabulous personality." Some day she intends to videotape him at home so everyone who has seen him in public can see what he's like when he really relaxes.

He and Beth, the "brood mom" dog, are joined at the hip. They run and play, often quite roughly with each other. The two of them will play catch together, or grab a stuffed toy and play with it in the yard, one digging the hole, the other burying the toy. "Beth, I believe, has done the most in helping Blast come out of his shell," says Judy.

He's still a work in progress, and Judy continues to push his comfort zone. "I do take him out to social events, because he needs that. He vibrates when we first get somewhere, but eventually he stops shaking and stands there—still very wary, still very aware of his surroundings. But it's something he can work through for short periods."

So when Judy awoke to find him on her bed, she knew they'd made the biggest breakthrough yet. "It's almost unbelievable when I look back to where he came from. He's up on a bed, with a *human* in it!"

Blaster was afraid to race. He was afraid to face the world. But, for Judy, he learned to let himself be loved. "The best part for me, now that he has learned the joy of human contact, is that hugging is great!" she says. "No dog should die without being hugged."

Wheels for Lewis

IT'S A SCORCHING SUMMER WEEKEND in Burnaby, BC, without even the barest whisper of a breeze to lift the heat. The distant, snow-topped mountains seem like a mirage (or wishful thinking) to the spectators fanning themselves in the stands at the annual K9 Cliffhangers agility trial. The heat, at 34 degrees Celsius, is even worse for the competitors. But as Anna Lupacchino approaches the start line with Lewis, her "All Canadian" mixed-breed dog, the only thing on her mind is teamwork. She and Lewis must be like dancers, perfectly in step, predicting each move a split second before it happens. Anna signals Lewis to wait while she gets into position. Then, she motions him to begin and they both start running. Lewis vaults over obstacles, races through tunnels, goes up and over the A-frame and the teeter-totter—exactly where Anna directs him. When they cross the finish line, the crowd goes crazy. People leap to their feet with applause and cheers. Anna throws her arms around Lewis, and he slathers her face with kisses. "Since family, friends and clients were there to watch, it was really important to me," explains Anna. "Lewis knew it too, and he did particularly well, even with the heat."

Although Lewis had only been competing for four years, Anna knew they could do it. That May, Lewis had earned his Agility Trial Champion Canada title, and only days later they had competed at the BC/Yukon Regional Agility Championships in Kamloops. The heat was so intense that weekend that dogs were being hosed down between runs. Anna, who also competes with two more experienced dogs, Zeena and Brutus, wasn't expecting stellar performances from any of them, given the weather. "I was just overjoyed that all three of my dogs had run well and, in particular, that Lewis had run clean and done all his gambles," she says. "Gamblers" courses require dogs to work away from their handlers, something many dogs find difficult. For a relatively new dog, it's a big achievement, and Anna was justifiably pleased, but she wasn't even paying attention to the scores until someone nudged her. "A fellow competitor in my class, Sonya, came to me and said, 'Anna, I think Lewis did it—he's number one.' I said something like, '*What*!!!' and then I specifically remember leaping into her arms." It got better:

Lewis in competition

Zeena took first place in her class, and Brutus took fifth place. "They all got steak that night!"

Lewis now holds eight titles with the Agility Association of Canada, and he's only six years old. For Anna, who teaches classes to beginners at Allstar Agility in Surrey, BC, he's her shining star. "After the regionals, my phone started ringing with people calling to ask if I taught agility," says Anna. "Lewis, Brutus and Zeena launched my career as an agility instructor to a new level."

Zeena and Brutus were still both young and challenging, and Anna hadn't planned on getting a third dog. Her husband, Scott, however, had other ideas. "My husband is the devil!" says Anna with a wry smile. "He thought I didn't have enough to do!" Anna had only recently become involved in dog training and was in Toronto at her first Canadian Association of Pet Dog Trainers conference. When she phoned to give him her flight information, Scott mentioned that he'd seen a puppy at the pound that looked just like Brutus as a puppy. Anna told him that they did not need a third dog and, although he really wanted the puppy, Scott didn't push the issue. The day after Anna got back, however, it was a different story.

"Monday morning he woke up and said, 'Let's go to the pound,'" says Anna. "We just had to go check out this puppy. Well, we did, and it was tough. I could tell Scott was totally in love with him. But Zeena was such a handful, I thought, 'I can't, I really can't.'" Zeena and Brutus were both high-maintenance companions, and she'd worked through many issues with them. What would happen if they threw a puppy into the mix? But Lewis was irresistible. They decided to give it a try anyway.

"Zeena and Brutus were completely unimpressed," reports Anna. The dogs didn't harm the puppy, but they let him know he was not welcome on walks, he was not invited to meals, and they were not put on the earth to entertain him. The dogs were so out of sorts that Scott, broken-hearted, finally brought Lewis back to the shelter. When he returned home, empty-handed and weeping, he just looked at his wife, shaking his head. "Do you want me to go back and get him?" Anna asked him. "I don't know," Scott answered through his tears. "You decide."

Anna threw on some clothes and raced back to the shelter. The puppy was still there, but the woman in charge of adoptions was out for lunch. While Anna waited, she was given permission to sit with Lewis. "I took him out to a park bench and put him in my lap. I said, 'You'd better be a good little dog, because I can't do this if you're not.' He just looked at me, and it was as if he were speaking to me. The clouds parted and the sun shone down on us. It was bizarre." She decided the universe was giving her a sign. This puppy was meant to be with them. "I know it sounds corny," admits Anna, "but it's totally the way it happened. He looked at me with the most soulful eyes and I felt his comfort when he was in my arms." So Lewis came home, this time for good.

"It was a turning point," remembers Anna. "From that day forward, Zeena and Brutus were far more accepting." Harmony returned, and the two older dogs even took on the job of teaching the young pup what was expected of him. Lewis quickly learned to follow them around the house and mimic their behaviour. "Brutus and Zeena made my job training Lewis easy," she adds.

Although Anna had always loved dogs, her first career was working as a legal assistant. Fourteen years of long days and too much pressure, however, left her craving a new direction. With Zeena's arrival in 1997, her schedule became even more of an issue. Then, during a series of obedience classes with Zeena, the instructor asked Anna if she'd be interested in working as an assistant. "I'd wanted to do behaviour work way back when I was a kid," Anna says. "I just didn't get to do all the schooling." When her instructor offered to train her at no charge in exchange for her teaching assistance, Anna jumped at the chance. "Every door in my life has been opened by my dogs," she says, "both personally and on a business level. It's been just amazing."

Anna spent two days each week helping teach new dog owners how to work with their dogs. Before long, people were asking for her by name. She was building her own clientele. She taught with a training company who had a contract with the Vancouver School Board. Before long, she was able to quit her legal assistant job and focus completely on being a professional dog trainer.

In 1998 Brutus joined their family. A young adult dog, he'd been relinquished by his first owners because of his unmanageable behaviour. Anna fell in love with him. All he needed, she felt, was the proper guidance. Soon he was her classroom model. Her life was falling into place better than she could ever have imagined. She had a husband she loved, two dogs she'd rescued and helped become wonderful companions, and a career she was passionate about.

Then Lewis arrived. "Scott wanted me to have an animal I could train from puppyhood," says Anna. "He believed in me as a trainer and wanted me to have this." When she and Lewis stood on the podium at the regional championships, amidst riotous applause, she remembered that decision.

Months later, she remembered it again.

One night, when Lewis was almost seven years old, everything changed. "It was February 8, 2006," remembers Anna. She'd been up late the night before, and Lewis had stayed with her while she worked in her home office. When she finally went to bed, around 1 a.m., Lewis followed her, curling up in his customary spot in the closet. "He's always been a really good sleeper," says Anna. "He snores and everything. He's in la-la land." That night, however, he got up at around 3 a.m. and came to Anna's side of the bed she shared with Scott. "I didn't open my eyes," says Anna, "because I didn't want him to think I was going to get up. I told him to go back to bed, and he didn't bug me anymore." When Scott got up a few hours later, Lewis was on a mat next to their bed, but he didn't get up. Scott figured he was just tired, so he left for work.

But when Anna woke up at 6 a.m., she saw Lewis at the side of her bed and realized immediately that something was very wrong. "His legs were not underneath him properly, but hanging under him, and he was dragging himself with his front paws," she says. He let her touch him, and he didn't appear to be in pain, but Anna almost passed out when she recognized the obvious abnormality of his appearance. As soon as her head cleared, she got a towel and slung it beneath his abdomen to help him stand up. Suddenly, overnight, her athletic dog was partially paralyzed.

"His back end was like a wet noodle," she remembers. "I kept saying, 'Oh my God, oh my God,' over and over. Zeena and Brutus kept circling around him, then racing back to check on me."

Anna scooped up Lewis in her arms, all 30 kilograms of him, and carried him downstairs. "I don't remember those 14 steps, but I somehow made it down." She tried again to help him stand, but his back legs were completely useless. She phoned Scott and begged him to come home. Then she called her veterinarian. "Get him in now!" they told her.

At the hospital, Anna's regular veterinarian tested Lewis' reflexes, over and over. They pinched his toes, they pinched his tail, they poked the skin over his back, looking for anything that would indicate that Lewis felt something. "They took pliers to his toes," Anna remembers, "but he had no deep pain sensation at all in his back legs."

The vet advised them to take Lewis to Canada West Veterinary Specialists and Critical Care Hospital, where the dog would be able to have an MRI and be assessed by a neurologist. The veterinarian put a pain patch on Lewis, partly to ensure his comfort and partly to ease Anna's fears that Lewis might be hurting somewhere else. But in her heart, she knew. "He wasn't in pain," says Anna. "Quite the contrary: he didn't feel a damn thing."

They sped to the facility, a state-of-the-art hospital filled with more specialists and equipment than some human hospitals. "You know, when people are telling you bad news, they're always very diplomatic," says Anna. "My dogs have taught me well to observe body language. From the way the veterinarian and the neurologist kept looking at each other, I just knew this was not good."

The MRI showed that Lewis had intervertebral disc disease. The discs, little pillow-like structures, sit between the vertebrae, giving the spine flexibility and keeping the bones from touching each other. But when a disc ruptures, it can cause havoc. Lewis' problems resulted from disc material pushing against the spinal cord, damaging the nerves. The neurologist recommended surgery, hoping the nerves might regenerate if the disc material was removed. Anna and Scott didn't think twice. "We were told we'd caught it early and that current thinking is to intervene quickly to remove the disc material, removing the pressure from the spinal cord. Hopefully, he'd walk again."

Anna and Scott handed over their credit card, kissed Lewis and left. "We never ever considered euthanasia," says Anna. "How could we think of it? This is a dog that has given so much, so unconditionally, I couldn't just give up on him. He's been my shadow. I'm never alone, because Lewis is always with me. He's my class assistant and my students' inspiration. He's my agility teammate, my walking partner—he always walks behind me on my right side, never ahead. He's my playmate at the park, my camping buddy, my cuddle partner. We knew we had to try anything and everything."

It would be a long surgery, and they were advised to go

home and return the next day. Anna had a class to teach that evening, and she went to it and taught, saying nothing to her students about Lewis. She knew that if she started talking, she'd fall apart.

"The next day we were allowed to see him, and it was horrendous," she says. "They took us into a little room. He had staples everywhere, in a straight line from his front legs all the way down to his tailbone. It's the scariest thing I've ever seen." The surgeons explained that once they got inside, they discovered that the damage was far more extensive than they'd anticipated. Anna and Scott should not expect any improvement in Lewis' condition. "We could see him a couple of times a day, for half an hour at a time. The first time, it was really shocking," Anna admits. "I cried."

Word of Lewis' condition quickly spread among Anna's clients and students, and people began dropping by the clinic to bring gifts and encouragement. "He had so many visitors," remembers Anna. People brought toys for Lewis, and some even chipped in to help defray Lewis' medical expenses. "That's when I realized how many hearts Lewis has touched," says Anna. "One client I hadn't seen for a couple of years, Val Tulman, set up a fundraising drive called 'For the Love of Lewis.'"

Finally, Lewis came home, and they set about adjusting to their new life. Anna took Lewis for acupuncture sessions. They began physiotherapy sessions at a canine sports medicine facility called The Spaw, where dogs with mobility problems use an underwater treadmill to exercise their limbs weightlessly. She did range-of-motion exercises with him. Finally, she had to face the harsh reality: Lewis was not going to get better.

"When Lewis came home from Critical Care," says Anna, "Brutus took over the role Lewis had played. It was amazing. Lewis had always followed me around the house, but he was too weak and had to have crate rest, so Brutus started following me around. Every time I turned around, Brutus was there, in the same room with me, underfoot. He had never done this before." Throughout the many caretaking tasks Lewis required, Brutus was there, lying next to Lewis, watching what Anna was doing. "He followed me outside in the middle of the night and stood by me while I expressed Lewis' bladder," says Anna. "I even ended up locking Brutus outside one night. I hadn't seen him come out with me, mostly because I was so dead tired." When she woke up two hours later to take Lewis out to the backyard again, there was Brutus sitting at the back door, waiting patiently to be let back inside. That's when Anna realized what Brutus was doing—he was helping her take care of Lewis.

Anna and Scott were in the middle of renovating their bedroom when this all began, so when Lewis first came home, Anna slept downstairs in their spare bedroom with him. When the work was finally done, two weeks later, Anna took the bedding back upstairs and set up a comfortable nest for Lewis. The first night, Scott carried him up and settled him in for the night. In the morning, he helped Lewis downstairs for breakfast. The next night, however, when Anna called Lewis to the stairs for bedtime, he refused to come. "He just looked at me, and then "ran" to his bed in the downstairs bedroom. I've never seen a dog run so fast on two legs." Scott told her not to worry about it, that Lewis just didn't like the hardwood. He couldn't get a purchase on the slippery surface with his front paws. Lewis would be fine sleeping by himself, he reassured his wife. "I was crying and arguing," Anna says. "Then Brutus came over to me and nudged me."

Brutus went over to the bed where Lewis had plopped himself and lay down right next to him. Anna never for a moment thought that he intended to sleep there. She went upstairs to get ready for bed, confident that as soon as Brutus heard them moving around, he'd join them again. But he didn't. "He didn't get up," she says. "He didn't move. He stayed with Lewis and babysat him all night." Every night since then, he makes sure Lewis is settled comfortably, then comes up to sleep with Anna and Scott. First thing in the morning, he dashes downstairs to be with Lewis.

Brutus also guards Lewis when the dogs meet up with strangers on their daily walks. "When dogs come rushing up to greet them, Brutus gets in between Lewis and the stranger," explains Anna. "It's like he's saying, 'Okay, enough already. Leave my brother alone. He can't defend himself.'"

Zeena dealt with things in her own way. "She's a very playful dog and can roughhouse with the best of them," Anna says, "but she makes sure she wears kid gloves with Lewis. It's really interesting to see the dynamics of their relationship. She knows she shouldn't play rough, so she has become very soft and gentle with him."

"Within a month of the surgery," says Anna, "our vet said, 'He's not going to walk again. You need to think about getting him a cart to get around in. He's young. He needs to live his life.' I totally agreed with him." Lying on a mat, day in and day out, would be no life at all for a dog as active as Lewis had been.

Staff at The Spaw directed Anna to a company that makes equipment for handicapped pets. Specially designed carts, she discovered, allow paraplegic animals to walk while protecting their paralyzed limbs from accidental injury. For Lewis, who'd been an athlete, perhaps this would return some quality of life. Anna immediately knew how she'd use the money her friends had collected for her. "Two swim sessions and his cart were basically paid for by donations," she says. They placed an order and anxiously awaited its arrival. When she saw it, Anna knew it was exactly what Lewis needed. The cart is a simple, two-wheeled device that holds the back legs securely, in a natural position, allowing the dog to pull himself along by his front legs. Lewis' cart has large rubber bike tires for manoeuvrability and speed. "He can sure go places in his cart," says Anna. "Through

Lewis' cart gives him mobility

trails, on the beach, in the snow, he even plays fetch at the park. A half-hour walk often turns into an hour because of all the people who come to see him and ask questions. Even the shyest of children in the park come running to greet him, to see how he moves in his cart."

In the year since Lewis became paralyzed, his care has gone from traumatic to ordinary. "It added a lot of stress to my life at first, but now it's routine," emphasizes Anna. "Lewis isn't stressed, I'm not stressed and the other dogs aren't stressed."

When it came time for the next BC/Yukon Regional Agility Championships, Anna considered not attending.

Scott convinced her that they needed to go and reminded her that Brutus and Zeena still wanted to run. Anna also knew that many of her friends in the agility community wanted to see them. Hard as it would be, she had to go.

Once she got there, it was even more emotional than she expected. Many top dogs had retired or passed away in the previous year, and a commemorative photo board had been erected on which people could write notes. "I couldn't bear to look at the board," says Anna. She walked among the stands, with Lewis in his cart beside her. People came up to them constantly, expressing their support and concern. It was touching, but exhausting. Suddenly, Lewis' ears went up. He'd seen something across the field. Before Anna realized what was happening, he bounded away, wheels spinning behind him as he sped off.

Since Lewis rarely left her side, Anna was caught by surprise. Then, when she saw where Lewis was headed, she was dumbfounded. "Robert Mallinson, a friend's brother, had become paralyzed while we were competing at the regional trials the previous year," she says. "I remember she got an emergency phone call while she was here, to tell her that her brother had been in a car accident." This year, Rob had come to the trials in his wheelchair. "Lewis saw him and just went running up as if to say, 'You're in a chair? So am I!' The two of them in their wheelchairs was an unbelievable sight."

No one seeing him as a puppy would have expected Lewis to become a champion agility dog. No one seeing him as a champion agility dog would have expected Lewis to become handicapped. Now he's an ambassador for pets with disabilities; everywhere they go, people ask Anna about Lewis and his wheels. "He's made it so easy. Seeing Lewis shows them that they can put a dog in a cart and go," she says. "He's not an inconvenience to my life. I love him enough to do whatever I need to for him."

7

No Punishment Here

EACH AUTUMN, AS THE MAPLE and hemlock stands of Truro, Nova Scotia, begin their annual colour change, a small group of women nervously review their lists and lesson plans. Although they are neither veterinarians nor dog trainers, these women will be hosting an all-day workshop in canine behaviour for 20 first-year veterinary students from the Atlantic Veterinary College on Prince Edward Island. Their topic: operant conditioning. Their qualifications: training in a canine program called Pawsitive Directions. Their venue: the gymnasium at Nova Institution, a federal prison for women. Their status: convicted criminals.

The inmates are in charge of everything: they have a budget, prepare the activities, organize equipment, plan the menu. When the bus pulls up to the doors of Nova early Saturday morning, the veterinary students pile out with their backpacks and notebooks. They aren't sure what to expect; some are curious and some are openly apprehensive. What, after all, could these convicted criminals have to offer them—hardworking, successful students? Future professionals!

They aren't given much time to think about it. Their hosts immediately warm them up with an introductory session complete with coffee, tea and muffins. Once the students are revitalized, the inmates immediately shepherd them into the gym, eager to get to work. They're also eager to show off their preparations; the room is festive with colour and energy in the form of posters, flow charts, diagrams and equipment, all illustrating the various topics of instruction, from basic theory to how to teach assistance dogs to open doors. Stations are set up throughout the gym, and students, divided into four groups, rotate from one area to another, getting a new teacher and a new lesson at each station.

Within minutes, all apprehension is gone; the students are simply in another learning environment, taking notes from the experts. At noon, the group takes a well-earned break, ready to eat the full-course meal the women have prepared for their students. Before they know it, the day is over. The women of Nova clean up the gym, flushed with satisfaction at successfully completing their daunting task. The students board their bus and head back to the island, filled with ideas on how to use what they've learned in their own lives.

"It is the most powerful day of the year," Heather Logan, dog trainer, creator and facilitator of Pawsitive Directions, says with pride. "The veterinary students love it. And the inmates love it too. For some of them, it's probably their first natural high!"

It all started in 1995, when Heather received a phone call from Corrections Canada. A new federal prison for women was being built nearby in Truro, Nova Scotia. They were planning to offer occupational training through a canine program of some kind. Would Heather be interested in creating this program?

"My first thought was, 'Wow! I'll finally be able to write exactly the kind of program I want to teach,'" says Heather. She'd been teaching canine obedience classes to the public for 25 years at that point and, while she enjoyed it, she often wished she could offer more in-depth training than a one-hour-per-week, eight-week course allowed.

Her program was approved. In June 1996, Heather was hired to implement it. But first, she had her own learning to do. "I knew nothing about federal prisons or working within the correctional system," she says. And her background was far removed from that of the women she'd soon be working with. For over two decades, her life had revolved around raising her two children (now grown), breeding generations of Labrador retrievers and building her expertise in the field of animal behaviour. "I take eight dogs to work every day—six Labs, one border terrier and a German shepherd," says

MORE GREAT DOG STORIES

Heather. "I drive a godawful van, and on days like today, when it's raining, it doesn't smell very good!"

Foremost among her canine assistants is the matriarch, 12-year-old Jazz. Next into the van are three of Jazz's nine-year-old offspring, Symbol and his sisters Hope and Drummer. Seven-year-old Jive is also Jazz's daughter. Finally, Royal, the matriarch's nephew, is the baby of the family at a year and a half.

"I'm also 'owned by' a Norwegian Fjord horse named Dreamer, a goat named Bramble, three cats, two cockatiels and a rabbit named Martha," Heather adds with a laugh.

Her life is one of hard work, fresh air, laughter and the knowledge that she is in charge of her own life. Her five-acre property is fenced to maintain order and to keep the inhabitants safe, but there is much coming and going.

A secure fence surrounds the campus-style clusters of buildings that make up Nova Institution, but that's where the similarities end. Despite its modern architecture and thoughtful planning, Nova Institution is, above all else, a prison. The women who enter its gates vary widely in almost every area: education, age, ethnic background, family status. The one thing they have in common is the seriousness of their offences. "They've done some of the most major crimes in our country," Heather says.

Whether a woman is sent to a minimum, medium or maximum security institution is based on three main factors: the offence committed, the risk that the woman will offend violently and her behaviour while in prison. Most women who have been given a federal sentence in Atlantic Canada go to the Nova Institution for Women in Truro, Nova Scotia. Women who have had their parole revoked also return to Nova to complete their sentence.

All Nova Institution staff members receive training specifically designed to enable them to work effectively in a women-centred environment. But some of their most effective therapists are the dogs brought in by Heather through the Pawsitive Directions program. The programming strategy that ultimately led to the creation of Heather's program is based on five principles: empowerment, meaningful and responsible choices, respect and dignity, supportive environment and shared responsibility. Heather wanted a program that would be good for the dogs, good for the women and good for the community.

But how could she accomplish this?

She decided that the first portion of Pawsitive Directions should be an in-depth course in the history of the dog, fundamentals of operant conditioning, dog genetics and breeding, and canine health care, grooming, ethics and basic nutrition. To maximize individual attention, Heather limits each class to five women, and the criteria for acceptance into the program are clear. "They have to have applied themselves, and they must have time in their schedules to devote an hour to the program each day," she says. One hour a day doesn't sound like much, but for women with substance abuse problems, or other issues for which they are getting help, dedicating an hour each day, five days a week for three months, can be a huge hurdle. Many of them have never dedicated themselves to anything in the past, but Heather insists on this level of commitment; anyone who misses more than two classes won't graduate.

"Phase one is three months long," she explains. "They learn to train using operant conditioning behavioural analysis, based on the work of Pavlov and B.F. Skinner." Participants practise on Heather's dogs with the understanding that if they complete phase one successfully, they can earn the opportunity to work with their own dogs.

Heather invites Truro community members to become involved in various aspects of the program as well. Local veterinarians teach classes in first aid, preventative care, common diseases and signs of illness. A professional groomer teaches general grooming, bathing and nail care. "Various Canadian Kennel Club breeders come in to speak on their particular breed and to explain why we choose the breeds we do," says Heather. "They also touch on responsibility and ethics. A nutritionist comes in to speak on canine nutrition and talks about fads versus facts. We have a geneticist come in to teach basic genetics. And we also teach the women public speaking and presentation."

"Each woman is assigned one of my dogs," she says. "She has to train the dog to perform a chain of behaviours involving three or more behaviours linked together with one cue."

For instance, the act of retrieving an object is actually a series of linked actions: going to the object, picking it up, carrying it back and giving it up. The trainer might start by putting the object in the dog's mouth and rewarding him when he spits it out. In what's referred to as "backward chaining," she keeps adding steps until the dog understands that a single cue—"fetch"—refers to the entire chain of actions.

"When she's accomplished that," says Heather, "the trainer gives a speech at graduation to our audience of other inmates and staff about what she learned in the program and how she went about training her dog to do this behaviour. This is where the second of Heather's goals for the program comes into play: the women begin to gain confidence, self-esteem and a sense of responsibility." Each will, in essence, be giving a lecture explaining the practical application of behavioural psychology. "Most of these women have never had the opportunity in school to learn public speaking," she notes. "They've never taken part in a church concert, or a school music festival or anything like that."

Most of the women enter the program simply because they want to be with the dogs. "They all just love dogs! They tell me they have a dog at home, or they used to have a dog, or they always wanted a dog. Little do they know what *I* have planned," Heather says. "*My* goal is to build a little bit of responsibility, to build problem recognition and solving skills."

The other unspoken goal of that first three months is

for Heather to earn the trust of her students. "Maintaining healthy relationships is a big problem for most of them," she explains. "As the bond and the trust develop, they see the advantage of graduating from the first phase so they can move on to phase two, where they adopt a dog themselves."

This is when it begins to get really exciting. Each graduate moving on to the second phase of the program is assigned a dog of her own to work with, usually one that has been rescued from a local shelter. Heather evaluates all candidates for temperament soundness before bringing them to the prison, where they will live with their handlers full-time for the duration of their training.

Phase two, obedience training, lasts for up to nine months and involves a tremendous commitment on the part of the women. "Right from the beginning I tell them, 'Yes, you're getting this dog, and won't it be exciting when this dog is adopted back into the community?'" Heather says. "There's never a moment that the women aren't aware that these dogs are being prepared to do a special job."

The women have their dogs with them whenever possible, and they keep them busy. Phase two dogs spend an hour each day in class, which includes training activities, lectures, videos and guest speakers. They also get an hour-long walk every day, regardless of the weather, and spend one hour in the dog park. The women are evaluated weekly on their handling skills, and the dog/handler team is reviewed at the completion of each training module. The women are also required to maintain a daily journal documenting their training progress and their dog's activities. Throughout the phase, instructors assess the dogs' progress, and at the end, each dog is given his final exam: the Canine Good Citizen Test, which ensures the animal is ready to be adopted into a family. When a match is made, the inmate handler works with that family, teaching them how to care for their dog and continue its training. It's a bittersweet success for the women, but a vital part of their emotional growth. They've come to love their dogs, and it's not easy to let go.

Loving their dogs doesn't always come easily, either. These phase two dogs do not enter the program as cute, cuddly puppies. The average shelter dog is an untrained mixed-breed male, about 10 months old, who has known nothing but neglect and who has no future. "They are usually large, uncontrollable, and someone thought they were no good," says Heather. The women know they are rescuing a dog from death row, and the realization hits hard. "This," Heather adds, "is where you start seeing the changes."

One of her phase two students was a woman named Rachel who had never owned a dog before. "She was a tall woman who walked with her shoulders slouched over, looking at the ground," Heather remembers. "She was good at public speaking, but she was very shy."

Although Rachel successfully worked her way through the first phase, she wasn't entirely sure the canine program was what she wanted; she didn't like the dirt, disorder and mess that came with the dogs. But she needed to fill her time. She did her work adequately and completed her assignments promptly. Heather sensed that Rachel was holding herself back emotionally, but other than that, there was no reason to deny her entrance to the next phase.

Rachel completed phase one in late January, the depths of winter, and got her very first dog in February. "The dog I assigned was about the size of a border collie, but was part terrier," says Heather. "Think energy! Rachel named the dog 'Sammy.'"

The houses of Nova Institution are set on a small hill. The day Heather handed Sammy's leash to Rachel, no one knew what to expect. The two jerked and bounced their way up the hill, Sammy leaping at the end of the leash, and Rachel nervously trying to control him without contacting his muddy feet. "Three days later, Rachel walked into the classroom, handed me the leash and walked away," says Heather. "'Where are you going?' I asked her. 'I'm done,' she said. 'I'm through.'"

Rachel had had it with this dog. Sammy, she said, was impossible. She'd tried to walk him, but he had dragged her through the snow and into a tree! She couldn't be expected to walk a dog that was making her slip on the ice and fall down in the snow and crash into trees.

Heather took Sammy home with her that night. But the very next day Rachel came to see her again. Right away, Heather knew something had changed. Rachel wanted to know if she could try again. Rachel had realized she didn't want to be the one who gave up on Sammy.

"She went from being a woman who walked hunched over, looking at the ground, to a woman who walks with her shoulders back and her head up," says Heather. "Her attitude went from 'I can't,' to 'I'm going to be the best behaviourist anyone's ever seen.' She got to the point where she could do anything."

Rachel also decided to open herself up to life, in all its earthy richness. Says Heather, "Even though her room was always immaculate, she no longer had problems with dirt. She allowed Sammy on the bed, and she was able to bath him, brush him, do his nails, clean his ears and do any necessary first-aid stuff."

By the time Rachel was finished with Sammy, he was trained as a therapy dog; this uncontrollable, former juvenile delinquent dog eventually went to a youth facility. "Rachel went from not speaking to anyone to being willing to stop and talk about her dog to everybody," says Heather.

Pawsitive Directions relies on training methods that reinforce appropriate behaviour instead of reacting to inappropriate behaviour. For these women, who are themselves learning appropriate behaviour, it is a chance to gain valuable skills while learning alternatives to punishment.

"We use absolutely no punishment," emphasizes Heather. "We have a sign that says 'Punishment Does Not Work!' Everything they do with their dogs is done in a positive way, so they have to figure out ways of rewarding the dogs for good behaviour." Most of her students, she says, have their dogs under control within the first day. "It's a rare woman who within 24 hours of getting her dog hasn't taught it at least four behaviours on cue, without using any punishment," she adds. "When I come back the next day, they're waiting for me to get there! They tell me, 'He's the smartest dog! You won't believe what he can do! I've got the best dog in the world, you know.'"

Women entering this program often have low self-esteem and little belief in their power to control their lives. As participants work through the phases of the program, they experience what it means to contribute to society by rescuing and training unwanted dogs. They also get to feel the thrill of seeing these unwanted dogs succeed in direct proportion to their own training efforts. The work forces them to practise self-discipline and teaches them how to set boundaries. They also learn how to end relationships in a healthy manner and how to respect the efforts and successes of others in the program. And participants experience, sometimes for the first time, a completely accepting, non-judgmental relationship. Those that move to the final stage, in which they train assistance dogs, are also exposed to another disenfranchised group, the disabled. Rachel, for instance, continued with the program after she was finished with Sammy and trained four assistance dogs for people with disabilities. She has since been released from

Nova, and is now working full-time as a dog trainer and a veterinary assistant.

In phase three, the women learn to train assistance behaviours, begin to teach public obedience classes and learn to operate a doggy daycare. This phase usually lasts at least 12 months and provides advanced training for dogs with the potential to be more than family pets. "It's a lot of responsibility," says Heather, "and big changes happen when the women become the teachers." On Saturday mornings, people from the community bring their dogs into Nova, to learn from a phase three inmate. "The day before, the inmate needs to have her lesson plan written out and she goes over it with me," says Heather. "I sit in the class and critique her, but I don't do anything else. After the students have left, we debrief on how the lesson went."

Not only does the participant have five students, five dogs and her supervisor watching, but all the other women in the canine program must attend the lesson as well, as observers. "They sit in chairs behind the public students, so they're out of the way," says Heather. "It builds the class leader's credibility with the other inmates; she becomes a teacher in the eyes of the other students as well as the public. That's where the public-speaking practice really pays off."

Assistance dogs, however, are not trained generically. They work to assist one specific person with specific needs. But each time a dog is ready to move on to phase three, someone always seems to be there already, waiting in the wings for just such a dog. "The right disabled people kind of just appear when we need them," says Heather. "They call me and say 'I have this disability. Could you train a dog for me?' Then they come in to Nova for an interview."

All the trainers sit in on the interview, which is lengthy and very detailed. "This interview is the first 'face-to-face' moment in which the woman sees her dog is going to do something special," says Heather. The questions are very pointed. What is their disability? What would they like the dog to do for them? "We need them to elaborate as much as they can," explains Heather. "At first, all they want is a friend." But during the discussion, they discover that this canine companion might also be able to sleep on the outside of their bed to keep them from falling out, or bring them the telephone, or help them on with their socks or pull their wheelchair. "At that interview, women from phase two also see what their dogs could do for someone," she adds.

These dogs are taught special skills, including picking up dropped objects, carrying messages between people, pulling up bed linens, turning lights on and off, alerting to specific noises and assisting with rising or walking. Sometimes, they don't know at first how, or even if, a dog will be able to assist the person in question.

One of Heather's favourite success stories started out at the Lillian Albion Animal Shelter in Amherst, Nova Scotia. "I was at the shelter, behaviour-testing a bunch of dogs, and came across Ginger, a little brown dog weighing about

18 kilograms," she says. She doesn't often come across female dogs, especially small ones, so she decided to take her. The owner's reason for dumping her was that she was "no good because she kept getting pregnant." Ginger was an immediate hit. Since no one knows her breed, they called her "a purebred little brown Amherst dog." As soon as she was spayed and vaccinated, they started working with her.

Within a couple of days, Heather got a call from the shelter. One of Ginger's daughters had just come in. The owner heard that his friend had gotten rid of the mother, so he wanted to get rid of his dog too. "I was willing to take her sight unseen," says Heather. "The women took one look at her and said, 'Her name has to be Spice.'" Within a couple of days, the shelter called yet again, about another daughter. Like their mother, both these six-month-old littermates were dropped off at the shelter because their owners didn't want the inconvenience of puppies, but refused to have their dogs spayed. "Now we had Ginger, Spice and Sage," says Heather with a laugh. "All 'purebred little brown Amherst dogs.'"

And all, as it turned out, were immensely talented. Spice was trained to look after a little boy with autism, Sage went to live with a gentleman suffering the after-effects of polio and Ginger got matched up with May, a 13-year-old girl with cerebral palsy and epilepsy. "May is in a motorized wheelchair that she controls with a joystick," says Heather. "She has very limited movement and no verbal skills. She's strapped into the chair because she'd fall out otherwise. But she has the biggest, brightest eyes and an absolutely brilliant mind trapped inside this body."

When May and her parents first came to Nova, Heather couldn't imagine what a dog might be able to do for her, other than be a well-trained companion. Without movement, or the ability to speak, how could May give commands? How could the women train Ginger to respond to a girl like May?

"But this amazing little dog took on the job like magic," says Heather. "The trainers working with Ginger did an incredible job." They taught Ginger the vital skill of recognizing the specific movements that indicated May was about to have a seizure. When May behaved this way, Ginger learned to grab a cue card attached to the chair and run to the nearest adult. The card says "Please help, I am having a seizure."

"We all just fell in love with May," says Heather. "She's an incredible little girl, and Ginger's an incredible dog." Little by little, Ginger learned other ways to help her new friend. She sleeps with May at night, so that if a seizure occurs, she can keep May from falling out of bed. If May drops something, like her special spoon or fork, Ginger picks it up and puts it right in her lap, where May can reach it. The little dog has taken on a big task and has done it better than anyone could have imagined. "Ginger has been trained to work next to this big automated wheelchair in the position where she can't get hurt and yet is able to remain right next to May," says Heather.

"Phase three isn't the end," says Heather. "One more thing can happen." Graduates of phase three can apply to become Heather's assistant. The job, a paid position, involves helping teach the phase one and two classes and generally assisting with anything that happens in Heather's absence. This person also acts as an ambassador, conducting tours and explaining the program to visitors, who are often prominent community members such as teachers, politicians and judges. "This is a plum job, a coveted position," Heather explains, "and only one person at a time can have it."

By the time phase three is completed, the women have undergone tremendous personal growth. But the joy of sending "their" fully trained dogs out into the community forces them to say goodbye, a difficult task for those who have known only unsatisfying relationships. "These women have had terrible abuse and know what it's like to hurt and to be the underdog," says Heather. "In phase two, they start learning that there's more to life than themselves and become able to talk about how the dog feels. By the time they're in phase three, they're so used to showing empathy to the dogs that when they're working with the disabled person, they're very empathetic."

When the families of disabled children come for train-ing, another important thing happens: the women are able to interact with men in a new way. Some of them have never seen fathers that love their children, husbands that love their wives or men who treat women as people. "They are seeing functional families, which is new for most of them," says Heather. "They get to see families working through difficulties."

Through it all, Heather's main goal is not to teach the women in her classes to be dog trainers. "I was put here on earth to be a mother," she says with a laugh, "but I'm not hired by Corrections Canada to be a mother, so I work on cognitive living skills with every woman, every day." Underscoring each task within the dog program are much bigger skills: problem recognition, problem solving, facts versus opinions, consequences, responding to the feelings of others, goal-setting, attitude, initiative, and the most important one, setting the environment for success. "Those are *my* goals," Heather says. "*They* think they're just doing dog class, but really, they're learning another way of life."

The Flyball Dog
That Almost Wasn't

GWEN DINGEE ROUNDED THE LAST corner on the agility course and came to a stop. Dust swirled into the air of the dirt-floor barn, churned up beneath the paws of her dog as he leaped over the final practice jump. Gwen hugged Cruise, her four-year-old border collie, tossed him a liver treat and hurried to the sidelines. They'd worked hard; now it was time to take a breather.

Gwen wandered over to join her fellow club members at the doorway to the barn, where they'd clustered around a female visitor who'd just arrived. The woman opened the back of her van and gestured toward the dimly lit interior. Inside sat several crates, each containing a dog. The woman was part of a group on Prince Edward Island that rescued homeless dogs. She'd taken her vanful of dogs to Gwen's agility practice in New Brunswick, a three-hour drive, in a last-ditch effort to find them new homes.

"They knew that the club I belonged to was practising agility that afternoon, so they brought them along to see us," says Gwen, who, with her husband Carl, already had three other dogs besides Cruise that kept her busy with agility and flyball.

But she couldn't resist looking. They were a motley bunch of crossbreeds, but each one had something in his eye that called to her. The crate in the back of the van held a particularly pathetic tricolour border collie named Lucy. Mostly black, she had a tiny bit of brown on her hind legs and her front and a narrow white blaze on her face. Only 10 months old, she'd been carsick the entire journey and had needed to be hosed off before she could meet anyone. She huddled at the end of the leash, trembling with terror, her wet fur plastered to a 9-kilogram body that should have weighed over 13 kilograms.

"They told me she probably wouldn't come to me," says Gwen, "so I knelt down to talk to another dog. But Lucy came right over to me, crawled up onto my lap and put her head on my shoulder. She was tiny, she'd been sick and she was scared out of her mind. I just about cried! I had no intention of getting even one of those dogs, but she was breaking my heart."

She learned that this little dog had been born on a farm in Prince Edward Island, but had ended up in a pet store. A family bought her with the best of intentions, but quickly learned they were unprepared for the demands of a high-drive border collie puppy.

This breed, reputed to be one of the most intelligent of all dogs, was developed to work closely with shepherds, moving flocks of sheep over large areas of rough terrain. They control the sheep by stalking and staring at them, always slinking around the periphery of the flock. They can be highly sensitive, even shy dogs, and do best with positive training. Because not all kennel clubs recognize the breed for show purposes, border collie enthusiasts focus primarily on performance rather than appearance. These are working dogs, pure and simple. Without occupation, they are miserable.

Lucy's previous owners had tried their best, but she spent her days alone in the porch. By the time everyone arrived home, tired at the end of their respective days, she was bouncing off the walls, raring to go. An evening walk was simply not enough to burn off her pent-up energy. They'd taken her to obedience classes, but they still couldn't handle her, and by this time she'd become very timid as well. The trainer, fortunately, was connected with a border collie rescue group, and when she saw the frustration and discouragement of Lucy and her family, offered to take her off their hands.

"They don't like to put dogs down," says Gwen, "but they were getting full. Since they figured this dog would be the most difficult to place, she was one of the first to be scheduled for euthanasia. But I thought maybe the right home would make a difference."

Gwen and Carl live in the country outside of Moncton. At their home, this dog would get a chance to be outside and to run and play with the other dogs. They have a fully fenced yard and a dog door, allowing the dogs the freedom to come and go at will. It was worth a shot.

"My husband told me I was out of my mind," says Gwen with a laugh. "We did not need another border collie. They're too neurotic, he said. They're too high-energy. The running joke is that Carl didn't say I couldn't *have* another border collie; he told me we didn't *need* another border collie, so I actually didn't ignore what he told me."

The rescue people warned Gwen that the heart-wrenching behaviour that had won her over wasn't typical for Lucy. "Apparently, she's not normally a cuddly sort of dog," says Gwen. "When we got her home, I saw they were right. She could not relax in the house, and she was in constant motion for about 20 hours of each day. We think she slept for about 4 hours each night." She hid when people came to visit. Everything scared her.

For months Gwen could barely touch this new dog of hers. "That Sunday we brought her home in the backyard on a leash and I let her go so she could play. She looked at me, and then she was gone, running just as hard as she could run. It was like she could finally go as fast and as far as she wanted. She just ran and ran and ran." The months of frustration and pent-up energy finally had an outlet. But was it too late for her to learn to trust people?

And where would they begin with her training? She knew almost nothing, not even her name. "But she did know the word 'no,'" says Gwen. "We're guessing they used that word a lot in her first home." She decided they needed to start from scratch, and since she didn't respond to "Lucy," they might as well change her name to something else. "I was listening to Bon Jovi at the time we were trying to decide on her name," remembers Gwen. "I looked at her and asked what she thought of Bon Jovi, the music. She looked at me and cocked her head, so I said it again. Then I thought that maybe she liked the sound of the word 'Jovi.' She looked up at me and that decided it."

She responded to her new name, Jovi. But as soon as they were over one hurdle, another one popped up. "On the first day we had her, we were feeding the dogs, and I quickly saw that she had no manners," says Gwen. Her other dogs knew the routine. They each had their own dish, they sat politely in their spots until it was served, and when they were given permission, they ate. Not Jovi. "I had her dish ready and she ran up to me, ricocheted off my stomach, dumped food everywhere and started eating off the floor," she says. This clearly wouldn't do. They caught her, cleaned up the food and tried again. Gwen put her in a sit position, made her wait, then let her eat. "I figured we had to start with a few ground rules," she explains. The next morning, she picked up the dish and braced herself for Jovi's mealtime onslaught. "I looked over, and there she was at her spot where I put her the day before, sitting and waiting for her food," she says with amazement. "My other dogs were also sitting politely, but I was shocked that one time was all it took for her to learn. I knew at that moment that we had a very special, very smart little dog, and if we could ever gain her trust and harness that energy, well, who knew what we could achieve together!"

Gwen was just beginning to recognize the extent of Jovi's two biggest attributes: her intelligence and her energy. They were the biggest reasons she hadn't worked out in her first home. Would they be able to do better with her? "She very rarely stayed inside our house," says Gwen. "She'd be outside running literally non-stop for hours and hours at a time. I totally understand how they can work sheep all day." Before they could start with anything else, any kind of training or fun, they had to let Jovi burn off some of that vast amount of pent-up energy.

Unlike most border collies, however, Jovi did not seem interested in playing. "We have a herding ball that she pushes around for hours at a time," says Gwen, "but when we threw toys for her, she didn't bat an eye. When we showed her a ball, it was like she'd never seen one before. What's a ball?" Most border collies drive their owners to distraction, wanting to play catch. Gwen shook her head in bewilderment; with all her experience, she'd ended up with the only border collie on the planet that didn't like balls.

Jovi had to learn how to play

Not only that, but she really wasn't interested in people. She wasn't interested in the other dogs. She didn't need or want their companionship. Jovi feared capture and easily avoided attempts to restrain her. But what about when they needed her to come inside?

Gwen resorted to a trick. "I put my four other dogs outside and let them all play together," she says. "Then I called the other dogs in and Jovi followed before she knew what was happening." Pack instinct took over, to Gwen's relief. "She wasn't ignoring us; she just didn't seem to understand we were talking to her."

As Jovi became accustomed to her new home, her issues

became clear. "She was scared of everything," says Gwen. "The electric can opener scared her! If we moved furniture, it bothered her." Even doing laundry set off Jovi's fears, but, unlike what they expected, it wasn't the sound of the washer and dryer. "It was seeing the clothes in the basket," says Gwen. "When I folded the clothes, she actually had to get outside. We thought maybe someone flicked a towel at her at one time, because she only has to hear the snap of clothes and she's just gone."

Being involved in dog sports, they knew Jovi would be travelling with them. But when the other dogs danced at the car door in excitement, eagerly anticipating an outing, Jovi did her best to avoid it. When she did accompany them, she drooled and retched miserably. "We slowly got her over that," says Gwen, "starting by just sitting with her in the vehicle. Then we drove down the end of the driveway and back. The next time we went a bit farther. It was a year and a half before she got over the carsickness."

The most worrisome aspect of Jovi's personality was her lack of interest in humans. So much of training involves working with the bond, the relationship, between dog and handler. How can you train a dog that has never learned to bond with people? She could outwit, outplay and outlast anyone, and she seemed to have no need for emotional connection. "She was this bundle of neurotic energy," emphasizes Gwen. "She ran everywhere, either at a fast jog or a flat-out run. She'd run up and over the back of the sofa while we were lying on it. Jovi ran just for the sheer love of running." Gwen had never seen a dog with such a constant need for motion. She would run upstairs to check on Carl, then downstairs to check on Gwen, then to the basement to find a cat, then to the living room to find another cat, then to the kitchen to find a dog. Then she'd start the whole routine over.

One day, Gwen noticed something that made her think. "Jovi would run up the stairs, ricochet off the wall, turn around and run back downstairs," she says. It was, to her experienced eye, a flyball move in the making.

The sport of flyball is simply a relay race for dogs. Two teams of dogs race over a set of four obstacles to reach a box, which when triggered releases a ball. The first dog catches the ball, then races back over the obstacles. As soon as he's back, the second dog goes. The first team to finish wins. A flyball lane measures 15.5 metres from the start line to the box, so the dogs travel 31 metres there and back. The dogs earn points on their team's performance, leading to titles in the North American Flyball Association. Points are determined by the team's overall speed. Mistakes, such as dropping the ball or missing hurdles, will cause that dog to "re-run," and as a result its team will most likely lose the race.

Gwen could hardly believe her eyes. Jovi, this un-trained mass of problems, already had a perfect box-turn. "I thought, boy, she'd make a great flyball dog!" If only there was a chance of getting her to join in the game. When Gwen had first brought Jovi home, she'd had a secret hope that this little dog would be her husband's new flyball dog. Jovi's problems had dampened these ideas; Gwen's husband let her know that this new project of hers was only reinforcing all his preconceived notions about border collies.

But socialization means going out and being part of things. When Gwen and Carl went to classes or trials or tournaments with her other dogs, Jovi came along too. "It was challenging," she says. "Jovi didn't want to meet other dogs, and she certainly didn't want to meet people. She just hid behind my legs." Jovi was never threatening; she was just obviously uncomfortable with anything unfamiliar. But Gwen persevered, taking her everywhere with them. After some initial obedience classes, Gwen decided it might be worth trying her out at agility. After all, her other dogs loved it.

"Jovi didn't like it," Gwen says. "She's very athletic, but you could tell she wasn't enjoying it. It was the slowest I ever saw Jovi move. Friends who knew Jovi couldn't believe this was the same dog that ran so fast at home!"

If agility bothered her, Gwen thought, flyball would be overwhelming. Many dogs who play flyball work themselves into a frenzy of excitement, and the game is accompanied by much screaming, yelling and barking. Although she wasn't very hopeful, Gwen brought Jovi to a beginner flyball class anyway. She thought perhaps Jovi might catch on from watching the other dogs. But after several classes, Jovi still hadn't even touched a ball. Unlike obedience and agility classes, though, the sport at least seemed to twig her interest. She watched the dogs race back and forth over the hurdles. "It's not that she was getting stressed and anxious. She just couldn't bring herself to join in," says Gwen. "But I decided to persevere." Between practice sessions, when the other dogs were taking a break, Gwen taught Jovi to run over the hurdles by herself. "She'd go down and hit the box. She took to that like a charm," says Gwen. She wasn't particularly enthusiastic, and she wouldn't catch the ball, but she was playing the game.

During one class, Jovi and Gwen were playing their version of flyball when something happened that changed everything. "I let her run at the end when the other dogs were done," says Gwen. "This time, there was another dog on the other lane. All of a sudden Jovi hit the box and came back like nobody's business. She still didn't have the ball, but she came back like a speed demon." They realized she was trying to beat the dog in the other lane. For the first time, Gwen sensed Jovi was actually having fun. So they lined her up against another dog and set them off. Jovi raced to the end and back, beating the other dog handily.

But she couldn't play properly as long as she still ducked away from the ball. She had the "fly" part. How could they teach her "ball"?

"We figured that for her, the race is the reward, so we had to teach her that she could only race if she caught the ball," says Gwen. They accomplished this by blockading her in front of the box. If she had the ball, she could run. Without the ball, she had to stop. "A few classes of doing that and we had a flyball dog!" she says. "It's like a light bulb went on. She looked at me as if to say, 'You didn't tell me it was a *race!*'"

That was it! They'd finally found something Jovi loved to do. "Of course, being Jovi, she was still overwhelmed by her first tournament." The milling masses of noisy people and dogs upset her so much that she couldn't focus. She shied away from the ball, missed hurdles and generally reverted to her old "Lucy" days. "She earned about 37 points," recalls Gwen, "but she still wanted to race so badly."

In spite of her abysmal debut, they brought her along for the next tournament. As it happened, one of their regular dogs was injured, so they ran Jovi as a substitute. "We figured we'd just hope for the best. And she was fine, running every heat as our anchor dog. She earned over 1,000 points in her second tournament." Jovi's time varies, because she only runs as fast as necessary to beat the dog in the other lane, but it takes her just over four seconds.

Jovi is heading into her senior years now, but barely slowing down at all. "She isn't showing the least bit of stiffness or soreness at flyball, and there's still only one dog in our club that can run faster. Now she will actually lie at our feet. She even gets up on the sofa to lie at one end. The fact that she lies down for a half-hour at a time is amazing."

As her confidence grew, her ability to trust grew too. It

took many years before Jovi actively sought out Gwen and Carl for affection, but now, at age nine, she even greets visitors and strangers, asking to be petted.

"She came along when flyball was just getting off the ground in our region," says Gwen. "Now, everyone in the Maritimes who races in flyball knows who Jovi is. She has been the fastest dog on our flyball team for most of her racing career. She's our 'anchor' dog who loves to race and has come from behind many times in order to pull out a win for her team!"

Jovi became the first dog in her region to reach 30,000 total points, earning the title of Flyball Grand Champion, and in 2004 this little dog that nobody wanted was voted MVP by all her regional flyball friends. It's a once-in-a-lifetime honour, and Gwen and Carl were thrilled to have it bestowed on Jovi.

And Carl's reaction to Jovi? He's the one who runs her in flyball now, and he's crazy about her. "She was everything he was afraid of in a border collie, but now he wouldn't part with her for anything," says Gwen. "She has won him over so many times! She shared her love of flyball with him to the extent that Carl became a flyball judge. Carl is a very active member in the sport of flyball in the Maritimes, and the 'Carl and Jovi' team are a well-known sight on the Region 10 flyball lanes."

Jovi has come a long way from a scared, timid little border collie that no one wanted. "I cannot tell you how proud I am of this little dog," says Gwen. "For me, to have been able to find something Jovi loves, something that puts that sparkle in her eye, is so special. She has overcome many obstacles and is absolutely the love of my life. I still get tears in my eyes when I think of how close she came to being put down—and for no reason, except that she had too much energy!"

9

"This is Blue and This is My Dad"

"THIS IS MY DAD. HE'S in a chair." That's how 11-year-old Kendell Kitt used to introduce Randall Kitt, her father. And why not? For as long as she could remember, that was his defining characteristic, the first thing anyone noticed. In June 1996, Randall, his wife, Darci, and their baby daughter, Kendell, had just moved to Cloverdale, BC, when Randall decided to finally ditch his thick glasses. "I had really bad eyesight and had to give up a lot of things I enjoyed, like dirt biking," he says. "At age 30, I got laser eye surgery, and I was so excited! I could see again! I could finally go dirt biking again!"

Four months later, he lost control of his bike and crashed. "I was out riding my dirt bike," Randall recalls.

"My front tire hit the tree first, and my head hit it next. Now I'm a C5 complete quadriplegic." Paralyzed from the chest down, Randall was left with the ability to move only a few muscles in his upper arms and his wrists.

After months of hospitalization and rehabilitation, Randall returned home, determined to be the best father and husband he could be. But what would that mean? "When you're injured," he says, "it's hard on everyone in the family." Life had changed irrevocably, not just for him, but for Darci and Kendell too.

"I stayed in the house because getting out of the house was not a possibility," he says. "I couldn't open the door by myself. I get around in my motorized wheelchair, but on a normal daily basis, I need someone to come in and help me. Each day before work, my wife had to set me up with the phone button and my water, but if I dropped something, I'd have to wait for my care attendant to pick it up, or dial the phone for someone to come pick it up for me. I was very dependent on people and restricted in what I could do."

Early on, he learned about the importance of water intake for quadriplegics. "I have to constantly hydrate," he says, "to prevent urinary tract infections, keep my skin healthy and prevent pressure sores. It's one of the things about being a quad that you have to be constantly aware of. It would probably be the end of me if I couldn't drink." But if he dropped his water bottle, he couldn't even pick it up.

His entire self-image changed. No longer a breadwinner, he now relied on his wife and little girl for everything. Not surprisingly, it changed the way he interacted with Kendell. "When you're a father and you're not able to get around," says Randall, "it's tough. You're quite limited in what you can help them with as a parent."

He got an attachment made for his wheelchair, a platform with wheels, so that Kendell could stand behind the chair and ride with her dad. They became a familiar sight around Cloverdale, Randall and his little daughter zipping along the streets together, laughing. But when they returned home, he'd once again be the dad in a wheelchair, the one who couldn't do things, who couldn't go places, who couldn't help out or play or wrestle on the floor. He yearned to care for his child; instead, his child cared for him. How would she feel about him as she grew up, when all her friends had ordinary dads? Would she feel self-conscious? Would she be embarrassed? He couldn't help but wonder, even though he's never questioned her love. "When she's with me, I'm just her poor old dad," Randall says wryly, "but she talks glowingly about me to other people."

While he was in rehabilitation, Randall had become friends with a man named Bob, who had even less mobility than he did. After they finished their therapy and Bob moved to Kelowna, the two stayed in touch. A few years after the accident, Randall learned that Bob had applied to a non-profit organization called Pacific Assistance Dogs

Society and had received a service dog named Bear. Randall and his family already had a much-loved dog, a German pinscher named Sister. While Sister was an excellent protector and companion for him, Randall couldn't imagine a dog actually helping someone in his condition.

PADS dogs go out to people in BC, Alberta, Saskatchewan and Manitoba, and the organization is located in Burnaby, BC, conveniently close to Cloverdale. Randall owed it to himself and his family to investigate further about an assistance dog.

"What does this dog do for you?" he asked Bob. "We're already a three-ring circus when we go to the mall with our power chairs. Do you need that extra added spectacle with Bear?" Then Bob came to visit and brought his dog, still in training, with him. "I saw Bear doing all these small and intricate things for Bob," he says, "and he's worse off than me. And each day, Bear was doing more and more for him."

When Bob and Bear completed their training, Randall went to their graduation. There he met a whole roomful of people involved with service dogs—trainers, therapists, puppy raisers and other people like himself, people with disabilities who'd become more independent with the help of a trained service dog. PADS' mission, he learned, is to raise and train dogs for people who are facing the daily challenges of life with a physical disability, or who are deaf or hard of hearing, in order to provide a greater level of independence and an enhanced quality of life. It was a revelation.

A lifelong dog lover, it struck him that perhaps a dog could be more to him than just a pet. "If I'm going to get another dog," he thought, "maybe I could get a PADS dog. Instead of asking a family member to do things for me, I could ask the dog. I was game for that."

He went home and immediately got onto the PADS website and began the application process. Randall and his family knew it was a lengthy process and resigned themselves to a long wait. "We'd waited about a year and a half," remembers Randall, "and we thought we had longer to wait. Then one day, when we were out at a nursery looking at trees, we got the phone call." A litter of 18-month-old puppies was ready to begin their final training, and Ron, a trainer at PADS, thought Randall might be a likely candidate for one of them. He and Darci looked at each other, unable to believe it. Something big was about to happen, something that might finally give them back part of their lives and their freedom. "I thought at the bare minimum that it would take some of the physical burden off my family," he says. "I hoped I'd become more self-reliant. But I never knew what I was in for."

Randall had been selected to begin training with a dog, but he knew there were several steps to go through first. PADS personnel put each applicant through a series of in-depth interviews in order to find out as much as possible and make sure they match each person with the right dog for them. Randall's dog would come from a litter of purebred golden retrievers that had been sponsored by the Royal Bank of Canada. When he looked at the photos, one dog jumped out at him, a big-headed male. "This is the dog for me," thought Randall. "He looks just like me."

When the day came for the two of them to meet face to face, Randall waited tensely. The first dog to come into the room was named Athens. "He came flying into the room and started investigating everything," says Randall. "I called him over, but he wasn't too interested. He was too busy bombing around the room." There didn't seem to be a connection, so they took Athens out and brought in his brother, Blue. Randall recognized the big-headed dog he'd seen in the photo. "Blue went around the room once, then came right over to me and stuck his head into my lap and looked up into my eyes," he says. "That was pretty much it. I guess that's how a match is made."

An intense two-week training period began, eight hours each day. The dogs had already received 18 months of initial training, but now they needed to learn to work together with their new person to forge a team.

"Ron talked to us about our dogs and started us on a whirlwind of lessons," says Randall. "It was a little overwhelming. At the end of the day, Ron said we could take our dogs home. That was the start: take your dog and go home."

Randall returned home that first day with Blue at his side. "On the first day?" was Darci's response. Yes. From that day on, Randall and Blue were a pair. Their first task was to en-

120

Randall Kitt and Blue

sure that Blue understood that his first and foremost loyalty went to Randall. Darci and Kendell were out of the loop, and it wasn't easy for them. "The first year, they couldn't pet him or show him any love," explains Randall, "because when I needed Blue, I needed him to drop everything and come to me. That bond needed to be built before any other bond could be made."

Blue immediately began doing things to help Randall around the house. One of the first jobs he took over was keeping Randall supplied with water bottles. "If I drop my water, he'll not only pick it up but he'll carry it if I ask him," says Randall. "Then he'll give it to me, or take the empty bottle to Darci. She'll take it, give him a full one and he'll bring it back to me. And it's not just the water bottle, he will carry anything—the telephone or a piece of paper, or even my wife's lunch bag when she comes home."

Today, over two years later, Blue has opened doors— literally—that Randall once thought would be closed forever. "He needs constant brushing up on his training," Randall emphasizes, "but he learns things every day." Before Blue came along, when Randall was dropped off after an outing, he couldn't even get inside his home without help. Now, Blue opens the gate for Randall with a pull-cord. Randall drives his chair through the gate to the elevator at the back of the house, where Blue opens the elevator door with another pull-cord. Randall drives in and Blue shuts the elevator door behind him. When Randall says "Up!" Blue runs up the stairs at the side of the house to meet him on the patio. When the elevator stops, Blue opens the elevator door, tugs open the door to the house and lets Randall inside. Once inside, Randall asks Blue for a fresh water bottle. "He tugs the fridge door open, gets a water, gives it to me and shuts the fridge door," says Randall. "He's working, and more than anything, he loves to work. He doesn't want to just 'sit' and 'down.' He wants to push the elevator buttons."

Now that Blue knows without question who's the boss, Darci and Kendell are allowed to interact with him. "Kendell's the one who grooms Blue for me three times a week," says

Randall. "She does his nails, hair and teeth, and checks him over for any sores. She also feeds him for me."

One of the biggest improvements for Randall since getting Blue is his social life. He used to go through the mall with sunglasses on, avoiding eye contact, pretending he didn't notice the stares. "Since I got Blue, everybody smiles when we walk by," he says. "I take my sunglasses off and mosey through the mall, maybe stopping if a young child wants to pet the dog. A dog like Blue is a big ice-breaker, a magnet. Everyone wants to stop and talk to you."

But best of all is how Blue has changed his relationship with Kendell. Her teenage friends flock around Blue, telling her how lucky she is to have such a talented dog. Instead of the girl with a dad in a wheelchair, she's the girl whose dad has a really cool dog! "Before Blue," says Randall, "she'd say, 'That's my dad, he's in a chair.' Now she says, 'This is Blue and this is my dad.'"

Epilogue

MYSHKIN ARRIVED DURING AN EVENTFUL season in our home. The same year my husband and I entered a new age category, we were hit with one crisis after another. Recurrent health problems left me physically and emotionally depleted. My career continued to stutter and stumble. My husband was dealing with his own issues: the sudden death of a dear friend, a spurious lawsuit, a property tax dispute.

And that wasn't all. Our youngest fell down while playing, and when she got up, her arm bones weren't in the right place. After a trip to the emergency room, followed by a trip to the operating room, she came out with a full cast and an empty stomach. One week later, our second daughter came to me holding her abdomen. What was expected to be a routine appendectomy, however, turned into a week in hospital due to a post-op infection. A month or so later, I was back in hospital myself, for more tests. "If I'd known we were going to be at the hospital this often," I told Ray, "I'd have gotten a parking pass."

It seemed as though everything that could go wrong did go wrong. Driving home one rainy night, I almost totalled my car. No one was injured, but three vehicles were towed away. When I finally got home that night, I ran a very hot bath, immersed myself and began to cry. What next? How much more could we take? We barely recovered from one problem when another one took its place. I'd reached my limit. I was falling apart and very, very afraid. In my logical mind, I knew that I had a good life, that bad things happen and that everything is temporary. But that's the problem with depression: it's not logical.

Here's the most important thing, though: it does pass. You just have to carry on, through it all, until the sun comes out again. So I let myself cry, and cry, and the next morning I got up to begin again. I cooked meals when I wasn't hungry. Myshkin and I went to agility class, even though I didn't feel like it. I kept on writing, even though the words were dark and sad and angry.

Finally, the storms surrounding us settled down. Grief eased and relationships smoothed over. Today, our girls are healthy, happy and growing into confident, capable, beautiful young women. Ray's neither suing nor being sued. Shelves in libraries and stores carry books with *my* name on them. My husband loves me in spite of myself.

My little, black, curly-coated distraction helped me through a difficult time, and, if one puppy is good, two must be even better, right? A year after Myshkin arrived, we presented our daughter Andrea with her heart's desire: a Cavalier King Charles spaniel puppy that she named Addie. Myshkin sniffed her over and growled at her a few times, but they've been best friends ever since. At least once a day, the house is filled with the sounds of wild growling and snarling, the thump of soft bodies against furniture and floor. They run and chase each other wildly, Myshkin gracefully leaping over Addie as she tries in vain to catch hold of him.

Molly tolerated the youngsters, even joining them in play now and then, but her increasing frailty daily reminded us that her time was running out. In the summer of 2006, she lost interest in food. We cooked hamburger, opened canned chicken and turkey, but still she got thinner. All she wanted to do was sleep by the fire, her fleshless bones and papery skin soaking up the heat. Although we weren't ready to let her go, in November 2006, on her favourite blanket in front of a cozy fire, we stroked Molly into her final sleep. Two weeks later, BC was hit with record-breaking cold, wind and snowfall and I'm glad Molly's final days were warm and dry, safe and full of love.

Dogs bring so much to our lives. Myshkin is smart, but

more important, he's emotionally intuitive. When I'm discouraged, he reminds me that to him I'm the sun, the moon and the stars. When I'm on deadline, he waits. When I get up, he follows me around the house, carrying a toy or a ball. When I work in the yard, he's at my side, digging holes and pulling weeds with me. When I return home after being out, his joy knows no bounds. If I scold him, he's devastated; when I praise him, he's ecstatic. And when I'm down, he forces me to do the one thing that can help: play.

Last weekend, Myshkin and I went to another agility trial, where he earned three qualifying scores toward his Advanced Agility Dog Canada title. When we crossed the finish line, I heard the cheers and applause that always follow a clean run. He's a brilliant, ordinary, incredible companion and my little prince. He's a poodle. He's black. And Ray was right: he's perfect for me.

Further Reading

Agility Association of Canada: www.aac.ca

Birchcourt Poodles:
    http://members.shaw.ca/poodledoris/home.html

Chinook Winds Greyhound Rescue Foundation:
    www.chinookwindsgreyhounds.org

Eddie's Wheels: www.eddieswheels.com

Handicapped Pets: www.handicappedpets.com

Kathy and Gary Gibson, Custom Canine:
    www.customcanine.com

North American Flyball Association: www.flyball.org

The Pacific Assistance Dogs Society: www.pads.ca

The Spaw Canine Sports Medicine and Rehabilitation:
    www.thespaw.ca

Trinity of Hope Dog Rescue: www.trinityofhope.on.ca

Acknowledgements

My sincere thanks to the people who so generously shared their experiences with me for this book: Kathy and Gary Gibson, Tim Sundstrom and Lynne Pyette, Krys Prichard, Judy and Jim Sleith, Anna Lupacchino, Heather Logan, Gwen and Carl Dingee and Randall, Darci and Kendell Kitt. Thank you also to my family, Ray, Stephanie, Andrea and Megan, for your support and encouragement.

About the Author

Roxanne Willems Snopek has been writing professionally for two decades and is the author of eight books and more than 150 articles. Her non-fiction has appeared in a wide variety of publications, from *The Vancouver Sun* and *Reader's Digest* to newsletters for Duke, Cornell and Tufts universities. In 2006, her novel *Targets of Affection* was published by Cormorant Books. Written under the name RG Willems, it is the first of a new mystery series dealing with the human-animal bond. Short fiction by Roxanne is included in the anthologies *Half in the Sun* (Ronsdale Press, Elsie K. Neufeld, ed.) and *Blood on the Holly* (Baskerville Books, Caro Soles, ed.). Roxanne and her family live in British Columbia, where she is currently at work on her next book.

More Amazing Stories by Roxanne Willems Snopek

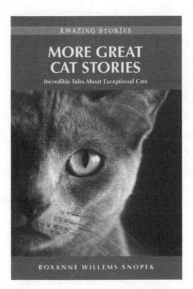

More Great Cat Stories
Incredible Tales About
Exceptional Cats

(ISBN 978-1-894974-55-4)

Great Cat Stories: Incredible Tales About Exceptional Cats
(ISBN 978-1-55153-777-1)

Great Dog Stories: Inspirational Tales About Exceptional Dogs
(ISBN 978-1-55153-946-1)

Inspiring Animal Tales: Heartwarming Stories of Courage and Devotion
(ISBN 978-1-55439-047-2)

Wildlife in the Kitchen . . . and Other Great Animal Tales
(ISBN 978-1-55439-008-3)

Visit www.heritagehouse.ca to see the entire list of books in this series.

Also in the Amazing Stories Series

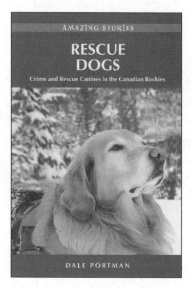

Rescue Dogs
Crime and Rescue Canines
in the Canadian Rockies

Dale Portman

(ISBN 978-1-894974-78-3)

This collection of crime and rescue stories by a retired park warden and dog trainer highlights the vital role dogs play in saving lives, upholding the law and recovering bodies. Portman describes the escapades of Canadian Rockies park warden Alfie Burstrom and his canine partner, Ginger—the first certified avalanche search team in North America— as well as his own adventures tracking down criminals and missing persons with his German shepherd, Sam. These stories will give you a new appreciation of working dogs.

Also by Dale Portman:
Riding on the Wild Side: Tales of Adventure in the Canadian West
(ISBN 978-1-894974-80-6)

Visit www.heritagehouse.ca to see the entire list of books in this series.